All the Best!
Tom Klobuchar

THE GENTLE LIFE

The Lost Art of
Being Polite and Grateful

THE GENTLE LIFE

37 Secrets to a Happy Life

Tom Klobucher

The Gentle Life—The Lost Art of Being Polite and Grateful

© 2018 All Rights Reserved, Thomas S. Klobucher.

Published by

NEXTIS PRESS
476 Brighton Drive
Bloomingdale, Illinois 60108 USA

No part of this book may be reproduced, stored in a retrieval system, or transmitted by any means, electronic, mechanical, photocopying, recording, or otherwise, without written permission from the author.

Limit of Liability/Disclaimer of Warranty: This publication is designed to provide authoritative information in regard to the subject matter covered. The publisher and author make no representations or warranties with respect to accuracy or completeness of the contents of this book. The advice and strategies contained herein may not be suitable for your situation. If legal advice or other expert assistance is required, the services of a competent professional should be sought out. The publisher or author shall not be liable for any loss of profit or other damages.

Cover and Interior Design: AuthorSupport.com
Cover Imagery: Shutterstock
Author Photography: Michael Hudson Photography

Hardcover: 978-0-9962609-9-2
E-Book: 978-0-9848469-9-3

Printed in the United States of America

*This book is lovingly dedicated to my wife,
Carol Klobucher, to whom I have had the incredible
honor of being married for over 50 years.*

*During our first conversation, I immediately realized that
this beautiful young woman was not only very wise and
fun-loving, but also an exceptionally kind and gentle person.*

*Our deep friendship, which still grows every day,
inspired much of the content of this book.*

TABLE OF CONTENTS

	Acknowledgments	*xi*
	Preface: The Fountain of Youth	*xiii*
	Read This First: Why I Wrote This Book—and What I Hope You Gain From It	*xix*
1	Follow the Golden Rule: No Gentleperson Ever Breaks It on Purpose	1
2	Be Grateful: Encourage Yourself and Everyone Around You	5
3	Be a Decent Person: Listen to Your Conscience	11
4	Be Polite: Learn the Language of Respect	15
5	Take a Breath Before You Respond: Don't Let Your Emotions Determine What You Choose to Say	19
6	Consider Silence: When in Doubt, Let the Other Person Have the Last Word	23

7	Focus: Give Your Undivided Attention to the Person You're Talking To	27
8	Laugh a Lot: Who Wants to Be Around a Sourpuss?	31
9	Respect Shared Spaces: Don't Monopolize Them With Private Cell Phone Conversations, Music, or Anything Else	35
10	Don't Use Profanity: Even if Others Do	39
11	If You Drink, Drink in Moderation: Respect the Environment That You Share With Others	43
12	Be Faithful to Your Loved Ones: Including, but not Limited to, Your Spouse	49
13	Dress Modestly: Modesty Is Always in Fashion	53
14	Don't Use a Sporting Event as an Excuse to Abuse Others: Don't Scream, Swear, or Berate Others	59
15	Choose Better Entertainment Than the Crowd Does: The Fact That a Movie, Song, or TV Show Is Popular Does not Mean It's Right for You	65
16	Make Dinnertime a Sacred Event for Your Family: Give Each Other Your Undivided Attention During This Special Time	69
17	Be Humble: Don't Boast or Brag	75
18	Know When to Forgive Others: Even if They Don't Ask!	79
19	Know When to De-escalate a Conflict: Not Every Battle Is Worth Winning	83
20	Know When to Embrace Conflict: Use Constructive Conflict Management Strategies	89

21	Be Kind to People Who Need Help: Be the One to Step Forward and Assist Them	93
22	Take Time to Pray: Communicate With Your Creator	97
23	Commit to Lifelong Learning: It's a Journey That Never Ends	103
24	Disconnect Now and Then: Be Willing to Disengage From the Wired World	109
25	Seek, Find, and Keep a Role Model: Be Aspirational!	115
26	Be a Role Model: Invest in Your Community, One Person at a Time	123
27	Give Financially to Charity: Offer Tangible Support to a Cause You Care About	129
28	Give Something Besides Money to Charity: Make Social Giving a Personal Priority	133
29	Be a Generational Translator: Learn How to Communicate With the Different Generations	137
30	Be Authentic: Never Pretend to Be Someone You Aren't	149
31	Be Tactful in Your Speech: Use the Best Words You Can Think of, not the Worst	153
32	Don't Talk About People Behind Their Backs: Work It out With Them in Person or Don't Talk About It at All	157
33	Be a Teacher: Share What You've Learned	161
34	Drink Deeply from Good Books—Especially the Bible: Books Are Among Life's Greatest Treasures	167

35	Respect Your Parents: No Matter How Old They Are	173
36	Build a Plan for the Future: No Matter How Old You Are	179
37	Be a Polite Driver: Put a Human Face on Everyone Around You	187
	A Final Word: Be a Witness—Notice and Praise Gentle Behavior Whenever You Encounter It	193
	Appendix A: Characteristics of a Transformational Mentor	197
	Appendix B: Ten Transformational, Life-Giving Steps for a Positive, Happy, and Engaged Life	201

ACKNOWLEDGMENTS

First and always, I want to give thanks to God the Father, who offers to us all the Fatherhood of God—the opportunity to be adopted into His forever family, if we put our faith and trust in Him alone.

My deep gratitude goes out to my father and mother, John and Rose Klobucher; my wife Carol, who is my soulmate, my partner, my best friend and encourager, and the one person who always makes me want to be a better man; and my two children, Lisa and Paul, and their families.

I am especially grateful to God for the memory of my oldest sister, Rose K. Kammerling, who saved my life and guided me as a young man to do the right thing, and who was always there for me in times of need. She was a solid rock of strength.

Thanks go out to all of the associates at our firm, Thomas Interiors, who make it a truly great place to work.

And I also want to thank Mike Cleary, my editor and friend, who guided and inspired me to stay the course on this, my eighth book; Stuart Hackett, my very competent assistant on this project, who helped me to stay on track and brought significant input and wisdom in numerous areas of the book; Jerry Dorris of AuthorSupport.com for the cover design and layout of the book interior, along with much advice along the way; my longtime friend Ed Hoover, who was the first person to tell me I needed to write books; and Ray Pritchard, mentor and friend; Lee Streater; Dan Sullivan; Daniel Wallace; Gerald Hills; and all the others who offered support, advice and encouragement along the way.

Special thanks go to you, the reader, for investing your time and attention in this book. As you read, my hope is that you will discover the great rewards of the gentle life—and that you will share what you've learned with others.

PREFACE

The Fountain of Youth

Before we get into this book's goal of establishing and sustaining a gentler world than the one we find ourselves living in now—a subject that has been on my mind for decades—I thought it would be appropriate to begin our time together by taking a look at the process of *writing* a book ... and examining why that process is, for me, part of what I call the Fountain of Youth.

This is a fountain that you can drink from at any time, whether or not you consider yourself a writer.

Let me explain what I mean. Almost a decade ago, in anticipation of my 70th birthday, I made plans to climb what the mountaineers call a "fourteener"—a peak of at least 14,000 feet. I did this because I wanted to challenge myself to do something I had never done before. It was a little scary even to consider that climb, and I got my share of nervous looks from people who loved me and had their doubts about whether I was up to the task. But I

The Gentle Life

believe life is for living, and I believe living fully means pushing one's own boundaries. So I made arrangements for the climb, accompanied by a guide I trusted. The mountain I chose was called Quandary Peak. It's near Breckenridge, Colorado, and it's part of a chain of mountains known as the Mosquito Range.

Perhaps at this point you're wondering: Did I discover the Fountain of Youth at the top of this mountain? Well ... not exactly.

I did complete the climb safely, though doing so was something that had seemed impossible just a few months earlier. What's more, I can tell you that reaching the peak of that mountain was an absolutely exhilarating way to spend my 70th birthday! One of the great takeaways of that experience was being able to confirm for myself that thinking I couldn't do something was no guarantee that I couldn't do it. After my climb, I felt like sharing that lesson with everyone. After all, it didn't just apply to me!

When I had completed the climb, the question arose: Now what? What can I do next to push myself beyond what I thought were the boundaries that I could never cross? (That's a great question to ask yourself at least once a month, by the way.)

The answer came fortuitously, when several people I respected and admired a great deal happened to mention to me, within a few days of each other, that I really ought to write a book about my life, career, and business experiences. I had never thought

The Fountain of Youth

of myself as a writer. I began wondering: Could I really begin a second career as an author ... at the age of 70?

Following those discussions with friends I trusted and respected, I decided to set another goal for myself, one that seemed like a truly audacious objective for someone with no writing experience: To write, publish, and promote my first book, *The Great Workplace Revolution*, within the next twelve months.

Taking on this goal was a lot like climbing that mountain in that it took preparation, persistence, commitment, and a good guide to help me along the way. It also took a lot of hard work. But, just like climbing Quandary Peak, it turned out to be possible, exhilarating, and worth it.

The process of completing that book was deeply fulfilling, and so was the reaction I got from readers. In fact, I got such a great response to *The Great Workplace Revolution* upon publication that I decided to set a few more "stretch" goals and create even more books, in keeping with a principle that I've been following for most of my life: **Everything I know, I've learned ... and everything I've learned, I share.**

With that principle in mind, I decided to keep on writing, publishing, and interacting with readers in the United States and around the world. In essence, I was launching a new publishing company.

Was one of those books all about how to find the Fountain of

Youth? Not exactly ... although, in a way, you could also say that they *all* were.

What I'm here to tell you now is that, nearly seven years after having challenged myself to climb Quandary Peak ... and write and publish a new book ... and launch an entire publishing operation—you are holding its eighth book in your hands!—I've never felt younger at heart, more alive, and more engaged than I do today. That's a great gift. I am truly blessed to have found my own Fountain of Youth—and, perhaps, to be able to help you find yours.

You see, I have been privileged to learn one of life's great lessons: We can all drink from the Fountain of Youth as often and as deeply as we want ... simply by challenging ourselves to do something we might have been tempted to think was impossible, and then taking action to meet that challenge.

I'm approaching my 77th birthday as I write these words. For some people, that's supposed to be called "old age." I'm not so sure it should be. I'm hesitant to say this next part, but honesty compels me to: I've met plenty of people who are twenty, or even thirty, years "younger" than I am, according to the calendar, who don't stretch themselves, and who have aged prematurely as a result. They're content to do the same old thing, follow the same old routine, and sit on the same old couch, day in and day out, week in and week out, month in and month out. They've chosen

The Fountain of Youth

never to stretch themselves, never to surprise themselves, never to challenge themselves to do something that seems uncomfortable. And they miss out on the opportunity to be as young as they can be, for as long as they can be.

Here's my request to you before we begin this book in earnest: Please don't be like them. Please don't grow old before your time. Challenge yourself. Find your own Fountain of Youth.

I can't tell you *what* it is—you have to find that out on your own, just as I have. But I can tell you *where* it is: It's just beyond the point where things feel comfortable, familiar, and safe.

Find it. Immerse yourself in it. Drink deeply from it!

—Tom Klobucher

READ THIS FIRST

Why I Wrote This Book—And What I Hope You Gain From It

"Civility costs nothing and buys everything."

—Mary Wortley Montagu

This book is all about the neglected art of becoming and remaining a gentleperson in ungentle times.

I started writing it when I realized that many concepts, rituals, and habits relating to what used to be known as "gentlemanly conduct" had been not only forgotten, but effectively reversed in contemporary life. Consider: Not so very long ago, it was considered unacceptable to swear in most social settings, to use public spaces as though no one else were around, to share intimate personal details with total strangers, and to take phone calls during dinner or other important family times.

The Gentle Life

These broad behavioral guidelines certainly weren't the exclusive property of the upper classes. There was a sense, shared by a large portion of the population, that violating them undercut society as a whole. Neglecting these norms was considered a breach, not just of etiquette, but of the basic standards that define civil behavior and enrich life in both the public and private spheres. Put simply, ignoring these standards represented a failure of personal potential.

I believe that most of us back then, in our better moments at least, liked to think of ourselves as "ladies and gentlemen" (for lack of a better expression). In other words, we liked to think of ourselves as people who knew better than to use profanity when giving a speech or presentation, or have loud conversations on crowded buses and subways, or mention our medical problems to someone we just met at a party, or stare at a screen with zombie eyes instead of socializing with family members at mealtime. Even if we weren't "ladies and gentlemen" in any technical sense, we could certainly aspire to that standard. The impulse to live up to that standard was, I believe, an important part of being a well-adjusted family member, a productive citizen, and, indeed, a human being others felt glad to share the planet with.

It doesn't take much research to conclude that too many of our social interactions today seem to be driven by a very different impulse. This book exists for the reason that our current tendency toward crassness, self-absorption, depersonalization, and a basic lack of respect for others seems so well established that we now live in a totally different world than the one I grew up in. In this world, navigating social life too often seems like a chore, like an endless invitation to stress, miscommunication, and conflict.

Although I'm not by any means the final authority on such things, I do remember a different way of living, and I know in my heart that living that way need not be difficult, even in the twenty-first century. In these pages, I've identified several dozen very simple ways that each of us can find our way back to the standard I call the gentle life—and reap the many benefits that come with it.

In what follows, I've opted to use the phrase "gentleperson" over "ladies and gentlemen" for two reasons. First and foremost, because too much of modern life is the opposite of gentle, and a reminder about that fact can't hurt anyone. And second, because "gentleperson" seems to capture the equitable gender relations standard of the twenty-first century better than "ladies and gentlemen" could.

In looking back at my own life, I realize that there were certain expectations people had of ladies and gentlemen, and that was a good thing. Ladies and gentlemen adopted standards of behavior that instantly set them apart from people who weren't interested in the welfare of others or of society as a whole. Among the ladies and gentlemen who surrounded me as I grew up, there was a willingness to observe, *at all times,* consistent standards of courtesy, respect, interest in others, and above all, a sense of common decency in public discourse—regardless of the social class one occupied.

I believe we now live in an era when even speaking about the importance of observing such values runs the risk of inviting ridicule. I welcome that risk, and I wrote this book in the hope that you are willing to welcome it too.

So here is the central concept of this book: **The responsibility for identifying and living up to clear norms of gentle (as opposed to crass and disrespectful) behavior within one's family, within one's neighborhood, within one's larger community, and within one's nation, is more essential now than it has ever been—and it falls on each of us.**

With that responsibility in mind, you will find here the specific behaviors that seem to me most essential for all of us eager to reclaim a gentle mode of life, in our own lives and in the larger society. This book outlines what I believe to be the essentials of the gentle life. I hope you find them helpful and useful, and I hope you will join me in using them to create a kinder, more decent, and more civil world for everyone.

CHAPTER ONE

Follow the Golden Rule: No Gentleperson Ever Breaks It on Purpose.

"Let everyone regulate his conduct ... by the golden rule of doing to others as in similar circumstances we would have them do to us, and the path of duty will be clear before him."

—WILLIAM WILBERFORCE

We'll begin with the "big idea" that supports every single syllable you'll be reading in this book—the idea that informs and inspires, not just gentle behavior, but a successful life as a human being. It can be found in any Bible, in Matthew 7:12: "So in everything, do to others what you would have them do to you."

This is the core principle for having a happy family life, for sustaining a successful marriage, for launching and growing a thriving business, and for maintaining any human relationship. And it's the principle with which we're going to begin our examination of gentle behavior. The gentleperson may not be perfect—none of us is—but he or she will never consciously subject someone else to behaviors or attitudes that he or she would not want to experience personally. To follow this rule, you must get into the habit of asking yourself a very simple, but profound, question: *How would I feel if I were on the receiving end of the action I'm considering?*

Posing that question honestly and with an open mind, reflecting on the answer that comes back, and acting in accordance with the deepest, most empathetic choice you can muster, is the essence of the Golden Rule. At the end of the day, following the Golden Rule means understanding that we should expect to be judged by our Creator with respect to our willingness and ability to put it into practice.

One of my favorite stories about this rule being followed in a practical sense comes from the world of baseball. Back in 1947, the president of the Brooklyn Dodgers, Branch Rickey, was meeting with Happy Chandler, the president of the National League, about a talented prospect the Dodgers wanted to bring up to the majors to play first base: Jackie Robinson. Robinson, of course, was black. Most of the major-league owners were dead-set against the idea of bringing an African American into the big leagues.

"We faced each other in my walnut log cabin," Chandler recalled, years later. "Logs blazed and crackled in my great stone fireplace. We needed that fire. It was a cold, raw January day. I told Branch, 'The other owners will never agree. You're all alone. I know you are here asking me for help. I'm the only person on earth who can approve the transfer of that contract from Montreal to Brooklyn. I have one question for you. Can Robinson play baseball?'"

"No question about that," Rickey said.

Chandler stared into the fireplace for a long moment, then said:

"Branch, I'm going to have to meet my Maker someday, and if he asks me why I didn't let this boy play and I say it's because he's black, that might not be a satisfactory answer. If the Lord made some people black and some white, and some red or yellow, he must have had a pretty good reason. It's my job to see the game is fairly played and that everybody has an equal chance. Bring him up. I'll sign that transfer."

In that moment, Happy Chandler held himself accountable to the Golden Rule. He asked himself how his Creator would want him to make the decision before him—and he asked himself, by implication, how he would want to be treated if he were in Robinson's position. In so doing, he became a role model for all of us to follow, demonstrating the extraordinary potential of decision making when this principle of Scripture is followed conscientiously by the gentleperson. Chandler's decision wasn't popular at first, but it was the right decision for him, for his organization, and for the country as a whole. We are all, to this day, in his debt.

That's the way it works when you follow the Golden Rule as the gentleperson's most important guiding principle. You end up setting the right example for others—by resolving to set the right example for yourself. In short, you make the world a better place!

WHAT DOES IT LOOK LIKE?

What would happen if you did something kind for someone who was recently unkind to you?

CHAPTER TWO

Be Grateful: Encourage Yourself and Everyone Around You.

"Even the darkest night will end and the sun will rise."

—Victor Hugo

Everyone knows the old saying about the glass being either half empty or half full. The cynic sees it as half empty, and that determines his or her experience. The grateful person, on the other hand, sees the same amount of water but draws a very different conclusion and has a very different experience. The question is, how will we choose to perceive what's in the glass? This really is always a matter of choice, and gratitude makes the difference.

Gentlepeople, in my experience, are those who make a habit of consciously choosing to identify something positive about virtually any situation—or at least keep the kind of open mind necessary to pose important questions about whatever situation they've inherited. Such questions include:

- What can I learn from this?
- Who could benefit from this?
- Where is the opportunity here?
- How can I express my gratitude?

By learning to ask such questions, and by making a habit of helping others to consider them, even in potentially difficult moments, gentlepeople make the world a better place for themselves and for everyone with whom they come into contact. They don't assume the worst. They assume there is potential, possibility, connection—and they work on the basis of that assumption. They are always looking for ways to become better people, even when that means accepting and coming to terms with seemingly worse outcomes than the ones they expected. They are content to let providence have the last word. They know that the real victory lies not in getting exactly what one wants, but in adapting successfully to what one has and then charting the next phase of the journey. This is one of the great accomplishments in leadership—and in life.

Think back on the people who have had a dramatic positive impact on your life, and I believe that you will find that most or all of them shared moments of gratitude that inspired you. In modeling and sharing the essential trait of gratitude, gentlepeople are a little like the schoolteacher who reminded her fifth-grade class that even at the scene of a major disaster, even in the midst of carnage and chaos, we still have the choice of how to define and frame what is happening. "Look at the first responders," she told her class on the day following a horrible news story. "Even when something terrible happens, there are always police officers and paramedics and firefighters who show up at a moment's notice, ready to risk their lives to help people who are in trouble. That's quite remarkable, isn't it? We can notice the injury and the loss of life, but let's notice that bravery and that commitment to help as well. The first responders are always there. No matter how scary things get, no matter what happens, there are always people who are willing to help. That says something about who we are and the kind of people we can be."

To put this issue in philosophical or perhaps even religious terms, gentlepeople are confident that everything happens for a reason. They know that even the seemingly difficult stretches in life contain important lessons and the potential for growth and new relationships. It's all a question of what we choose to make something mean.

The brilliant writer and psychologist Victor Frankl was a survivor of the Nazi genocide against the Jews. He found a way to give even that horrific experience—an experience whose dimensions most of us can scarcely imagine—a powerful and positive personal meaning. He decided that what he had gone through had happened for a reason. It had happened so that others could benefit from what he had learned in the concentration camp.

Frankl made it his life's work, his personal mission, to share with people a means by which they could discover for themselves, just as he had, the vital importance of creating a personal answer to a powerful question: *Why did this happen?* He wrote, spoke, and counseled along these lines for decades—because he believed that finding answers to this question could create meaning and a reason to move forward for people in any situation, no matter how painful and brutal.

With this mission in mind, Frankl once wrote, "Everything can be taken from a man but one thing: The last of the human freedoms—to choose one's attitude in any given set of circumstances, to choose one's own way."

Be Grateful

You, too, have a choice when it comes to the attitude you use to navigate the day. If you are a gentleperson, you will practice choosing an attitude of gratitude.

> ## WHAT DOES IT LOOK LIKE?
> How would your days look different if you regularly allowed yourself to dream about—and plan for—something beautiful that might arise out of a painful circumstance in your life?

CHAPTER THREE

Be a Decent Person: Listen to Your Conscience.

"There comes a time when one must take a position that is neither safe, nor politic, nor popular, but he must take it because conscience tells him it is right."

—MARTIN LUTHER KING JR.

Being decent is one of those standards that sounds vague, but it really isn't. All it means is that you are personally committed to earning the reputation of being a gentleperson ... by living up to your own personal standards of good behavior. Recognizing that you *have* such standards is the starting point. Deep inside, each one of us has a voice that tells us whether a course of action we are considering pursuing is decent or not. Each one of us has a conscience. Being a decent person simply means acknowledging that this voice exists—and recognizing your personal responsibility to follow it.

The great French writer Victor Hugo once observed that "Conscience is God present in man." He could just as easily have said that "Decency is God present in each human being."

Being decent means having a *consistent* set of personal standards that is in full accordance with your conscience. It means not going along with the crowd when the crowd is certain of something that your conscience tells you is wrong. It means being willing to say when, how, and why you are determined to walk a path on your own, because you know it to be the path of decency, the path you are meant to follow. Gentlepeople are decent, which is another way of saying that they have ethical standards from which they won't deviate, even when it seems popular to do so.

The following passage, deeply relevant to our discussion, appears in Harper Lee's great novel *To Kill a Mockingbird*. Consider it closely.

"Atticus, you must be wrong."
"How's that?"

"Well, most folks seem to think they're right and you're wrong..."

"They're certainly entitled to think that, and they're entitled to full respect for their opinions," said Atticus, "but before I can live with other folks I've got to live with myself. The one thing that doesn't abide by majority rule is a person's conscience."

There is perhaps no more decent figure in American literature than the attorney Atticus Finch. Ask yourself: What *makes* him decent? The answer is simple: Atticus Finch is decent because he refuses to ignore his conscience, even when others are ignoring theirs. That's one of the things that makes him a gentleperson. And following his example can make you a gentleperson too.

WHAT DOES IT LOOK LIKE?

Is there a specific action that your conscience is telling you to take? What would happen if you took action right now?

CHAPTER FOUR

Be Polite: Learn the Language of Respect

"It is a wise thing to be polite; consequently, it is a stupid thing to be rude. To make enemies by unnecessary and willful incivility, is just as insane a proceeding as to set your house on fire."

—Arthur Schopenhauer

Good manners seem optional to many people these days, but gentlepeople know that such manners are essential to our very humanity. As I was preparing this chapter, I was struck by what the great British statesman Edmund Burke once observed about these things: "Manners are more important than laws. Manners are what vex or soothe, corrupt or purify, exalt or debase, barbarize or refine us, by a constant, steady, uniform, insensible operation, like that of the air we breathe in."

Burke was absolutely right. Our manners are more important than our laws. And unfortunately, we live in a time when the manners many people choose to display, both in public and in private, vex far more than they soothe, corrupt far more than they purify, debase far more than they exalt, and barbarize far more than they refine. All you have to do to prove this for yourself is visit a busy coffee shop, watch television for more than half an hour, or check the comments section on the most popular social media posting you can find. As a culture, we are rude. We have lost our way when it comes to demonstrating good manners and elevating the standard of behavior that defines us as individuals and as a society.

I hope that it will come as no surprise to you that ladies and gentlemen in years past distinguished themselves and the societies in which they lived by their personal attention to the topic of good manners. Although these ladies and gentlemen may be less numerous now than they once were, you and I can adopt their standards and reclaim their legacy with very little effort.

Be Polite: Learn the Language of Respect

We don't have to memorize any elaborate rulebooks. We don't have to create any special clubs. We don't have to make any public attempt to change anyone's behavior.

All we have to do is make a habit of saying the words "please" and "thank you" whenever it is appropriate to use them. If we use these words in an authentic tone and accompany them with a smile, I've found that they have at least twice the positive impact.

If we do this prominently and without apology—and if we do so in interactions with people who aren't used to this basic etiquette currency—something amazing will happen. People will start saying "You're welcome!" They'll start using "please" and "thank you" more often in their interactions with others, following our good example. And who knows, they may even begin to raise their standards of interaction in other areas!

It never ceases to amaze me how few people—and specifically how few children—employ these basic elements of human politeness. We have fallen into the habit of taking each other's good will for granted. We have forgotten how essential it is to request things politely and to offer gratitude when we receive something. Making a habit of saying "please" and "thank you" consistently whenever it makes sense to do so won't solve all of our challenges on the politeness front. But it's a great start, and

THE GENTLE LIFE

it's something that will benefit everyone with whom we come into contact.

Will you please make a point of doing this today?

Thank you!

WHAT DOES IT LOOK LIKE?

Is there someone you might have forgotten to thank recently? What would happen if you contacted them right now and expressed your thanks?

CHAPTER FIVE

Take a Breath Before You Respond: Don't Let Your Emotions Determine What You Choose to Say.

"For every minute you remain angry, you give up sixty seconds of peace of mind."

—RALPH WALDO EMERSON

How many brutal misunderstandings, how many heartbreaks, how many needless permanent divisions in families, teams, and organizations could have been avoided if one of the parties involved had simply stopped to take a breath before responding to a harsh remark? This is a hallmark of gentlepeople. They don't react—they respond.

In other words, they spend a lot less of their time and energy speaking in anger than other people typically do—and this means that they spend less time dealing with the damage they've left in their wake! You've heard of the carpenter's advice: Measure twice, cut once. Gentlepeople follow a similar rule: Think twice, speak once!

It's a big mistake to let your emotions determine what you will say, especially when you find yourself in a difficult situation. It's far better to stop, take a breath, and let the calmest version of yourself survey the environment so you can determine what the best response is. The great humorist Ambrose Bierce once warned: "Speak when you are angry, and you will make the best speech you will ever regret." He was absolutely right. Too many people are in love with the sound of their own anger being expressed. They don't consider the consequences of "telling someone off."

These days, if you make the mistake of speaking when you are angry, you run the risk of having your words immediately recorded for posterity—and forwarded to employers or other

Take a Breath Before You Respond

authorities! Consider the following cautionary tale from the world of customer service. It really happened.

Years ago, a Microsoft employee who provided phone support for Windows customers took a call from a user who had a problem. She looked up the customer's record, and then told the customer that his support agreement had expired, which meant that Microsoft would be charging him for the service they provided during the call. That's not what anyone really wants to hear, of course, but it's also a perfect example of a situation where it makes sense to hit "pause" on a conversation, take a deep breath, and try to engage with one's conversational partner as an adult. Unfortunately, that's not what this customer did.

He went berserk, saying at one point, "That McVeigh, he bombed the wrong building!" The reference was to terrorist bomber Timothy McVeigh, who bombed a federal building in Oklahoma in 1995 and killed 168 people. The clear implication was that the caller wanted to bomb Microsoft! The stunned customer service professional, who knew the call was being recorded, asked the caller to repeat himself. The caller did! File under: "Ungentlemanly Behavior that Can Get You Thrown in Jail."

I don't know whether or not the threat was passed on to law enforcement officials. It doesn't really matter. The point is, this caller had clearly passed the point of rational discourse. Not

The Gentle Life

only did his threat have zero chance of attaining his apparent goal, but he overlooked the inconvenient fact that Microsoft had his address and phone number! Maybe the moral of the story is: When we indulge our anger, we lose valuable chunks of our civility, our sense of empathy, and our intelligence. Gentlepeople simply aren't willing to risk that. That's why they stop and take a breath, especially when they find themselves in difficult situations.

> ### WHAT DOES IT LOOK LIKE?
> Is there someone in your life you should take a breath before responding to? What would happen if you did?

CHAPTER SIX

Consider Silence: When in Doubt, Let the Other Person Have the Last Word.

"Silence is a source of great strength."

—**Lao Tzu,** ancient Chinese sage and philosopher

Did you notice that this principle is a continuation of the previous one? The ultimate expression of wisdom and discretion in social discourse—the final piece of evidence that one has paused and thought things through

The Gentle Life

before responding—is choosing not to respond at all. This takes practice, of course, but it is practice gentlepeople know to be worthwhile.

One of the great multipliers of needless, avoidable conflict is the belief that we deserve the last word in a disagreement. The cycle is a familiar one: We get so wrapped up in some convoluted argument that we may lose track of what exactly it is that we're arguing about—but somehow we don't lose track of the desire to get the last word!

This is an uncivil and potentially dangerous game. Gentlepeople, in my experience, know how to disengage from it. They know when the best and most eloquent response in a given situation is silence. They have moved past the habit of needing to have the final word, and they know that showing the maturity necessary to move on without comment is sometimes the best decision for all concerned. They're less focused on winning the argument, and more focused on the long-term relationship.

I'm not talking about using silence to freeze the other person out or make someone pay for a mistake you believe he or she has made. The so-called "silent treatment" is no way to treat anyone. I'm talking about dropping the conflict, dropping the desire to be right. This is an especially important principle to bear in mind when dealing with a spouse. An old joke—one that I suppose isn't particularly fashionable anymore—advises new husbands to make sure that the final two words in any marital conflict are "Yes, dear." Actually, I'd advise both partners in a marriage to at least consider following that advice every now and then. (Believe me when I tell you that, over the course of a marriage, you'll have plenty of opportunities to put it into practice.) If you're truly committed to the success of this relationship, that means you're willing to be gentle with your spouse, even if that means stepping back and letting the other person have the last word—and yes, even if it means being the first one to apologize. I've found that one of the guiding principles of a successful marriage is: The first one to apologize wins! (Actually, everyone wins when a heartfelt apology is offered.)

A good rule of thumb to consider following here is: If you think you've gotten the last word in the argument, don't let it stand! Apologizing promptly has had such a positive impact on my life and marriage that I have made it into a rule—I call it "the 15-minute rule"—and I'm inviting you to follow it, too. Don't let fifteen minutes go by without apologizing—and then be sure to listen for the other person's perspective and take advantage of every opportunity to validate what they express.

My last piece of advice on this principle is to remember the wise words of the great playwright Eugene O'Neill, who once observed that "God gave us mouths that close and ears that don't. That should tell us something." That's a great observation, one that's relevant to this principle. People who need to have the last word in an argument have simply stopped listening. They are effectively closing their ears. Don't follow their example! That's not how gentlepeople behave.

WHAT DOES IT LOOK LIKE?

Think of one or two people you know who seem to get you flustered or annoyed regularly. Would it make sense for you to be silent more often with them?

CHAPTER SEVEN

Focus: Give Your Undivided Attention to the Person You're Talking To.

"We do not find the meaning of life by ourselves alone—we find it with another."

—THOMAS MERTON

Today, we live in an era of perpetually divided attention. People are so distracted that they rarely look each other in the eye and rarely listen deeply. I think a lot of this has to do with all of the communications technology that's now available to us. There's so much "content" streaming at us from so many directions that it's easy to forget that there are still real, live people in our world—and that connecting with them when the opportunity arises is more important than engaging the digital world! It is and always has been an essential trait of gentlepeople to treat others with respect. When it comes to conversation, an essential component of respect is to give the person you're talking to your undivided attention.

This would seem like common sense—something that everyone would do automatically whenever a face-to-face conversation begins. Yet if you take a look around at the world in which we now live, you'll realize that it's all too uncommon. Think of how many times you've been in a conversation with someone who only wanted to look like he or she was paying attention to you—who was more interested in something on his or her phone, or on television, or on a computer screen. This is the plague of our time, and it has the potential to adversely affect all of the relationships it touches. The communications technology we have today is amazing—but when we realize that we're using it in such a way that it actually inhibits communication, we need to learn to switch it off!

At the end of the day, this principle is about the possibility of togetherness. That's what happens when two human beings connect in a meaningful way, and it's one of the building blocks of families, societies, communities, and nations. If we're not capable of togetherness, we're not capable of our best as people. We can't go it alone, and we can't expect YouTube videos to create actual, present-tense, face-to-face, voice-to-voice togetherness, because togetherness is all about focused attention. It's all about giving someone else your undivided focus. It's deeply wired into the human species that we have a fundamental need to connect with other people. Gentlepeople recognize that need, and they make sure to honor it by building focused attention into their interactions with others. They look you in the eye. They make you feel like you're the only other person in the room.

It is one of the great ironies of modern life that we are so often in the physical or even virtual presence of so many people on a given day ... but we rarely feel connected with people. If you think back to a parent, teacher, or mentor who had an immense positive impact on your life and consider what made that positive impact possible, I think you'll realize that one of the factors was this person's ability and willingness to focus on you with complete, unwavering attention. This is a determining characteristic of gentlepeople, and we need to model it more often in daily life—even if that means turning off the phone for a while.

WHAT DOES IT LOOK LIKE?

Is there someone you would do well to give your full attention to—putting away your phone, turning off the TV, and looking them in the eye? What would happen if you did it the next time you got the chance?

CHAPTER EIGHT

Laugh a Lot: Who Wants to Be Around a Sourpuss?

"At the height of laughter, the universe is flung into a kaleidoscope of new possibilities."

—**Jean Houston**

I believe the ability to laugh—and in particular the ability to laugh at oneself—is a major predictor of success in life, and I believe gentlepeople understand this principle and live their lives by it. Please understand that I'm not just talking about material success here, but about success as a human being. Understand, too, that the kind of laughter I'm talking about is laughter that does not come viciously, at the expense of another person's sense of self. Laughter that ridicules someone or makes someone feel small, under attack, or disrespected is the opposite of gentle behavior.

The great poet W.H. Auden once made the following potent observation: "Among those whom I simply like, I can find no common denominator ... but among those whom I love and respect, I can: All of them make me laugh." Gentlepeople know how to inspire this kind of love. They know how to use gentle humor to build bridges, inspire or deepen rapport, and create new possibilities of trust and connection. And they do it all the time. Some people call this trait charisma. I think of it as the willingness to use laughter to bring people closer together. The very best humor of all, for this type of bonding, is humor that makes fun of the speaker. This is the kind of humor at which truly great leaders excel. A classic practitioner of it was President Ronald Reagan.

If you're old enough to remember the 1984 presidential election, you probably recall that one of the major issues in that campaign was whether Reagan, who was in his seventies, was too old for the job of president. His opponent, former Vice President Walter Mondale, was about fifteen years younger. The

Laugh a Lot

topic of Reagan's age came up frequently in the media coverage of the campaign and was directly addressed in one of the live televised presidential debates. With millions of viewers watching, Reagan gently poked fun at himself—and proved to the country that he was capable of responding adroitly and sensitively in a potentially stressful situation—by saying, "I will not make age an issue of this campaign. I am not going to exploit, for political purposes, my opponent's youth and inexperience."

The studio audience roared with laughter, and that laughter echoed out across the country. Of course, what Reagan was really doing was acknowledging before the whole world that he was indeed the oldest man ever to hold the office of president, demonstrating that he was capable of finding humor in that reality, and, in the process, proving that he was still quite capable of handling himself in high-stakes situations. Thanks to his masterful one-liner, he bonded powerfully in that instant with millions of undecided voters, created a sound bite that would be replayed for generations, and effectively put the age issue to rest for the balance of the campaign. He won in a landslide that November.

Please understand that I'm not saying anything about politics with this story. All I'm saying is that gentlepeople—and Reagan was certainly one of them—know how to deploy humor when approaching a sensitive situation. That's a lost art in our increasingly polarized, increasingly serious world. We all need to take a lesson from the Gipper, I think. Nobody likes a sourpuss. There's no situation in life that's so serious that we can't find a way to use gentle humor to make it a little easier to deal with.

WHAT DOES IT LOOK LIKE?

Have you enjoyed a good laugh with the people you love in the last day or two? What about the folks you work with? How do you think people would respond if, every time you saw that they were trying to be funny and it was appropriate, you laughed?

CHAPTER NINE

Respect Shared Spaces: Don't Monopolize Them With Private Cell Phone Conversations, Music, or Anything Else.

"Public space plays a vital role in our world, equally important in our digital age as in Greco-Roman times, when they were marketplaces for goods and ideas. As common ground, squares are equitable and democratic; they have played a fundamental role in the development of free speech."

—**Catie Marron,** in *City Squares*

The Gentle Life

Break rooms. Subway cars. Buses. Storefronts. Hotel and apartment complex lobbies. Restaurants. Movie theaters. Each of these places, and dozens of others that I could have named, falls into a special category: Shared spaces.

I do realize that a lot of people might be more used to calling such environments "public spaces," but I prefer "shared spaces" for the simple reason that, these days, the word "public" seems to imply that anything goes! Gentlepeople know otherwise, of course.

The fact that we share the same environment with others can make it easier for us to begin an important discussion about respecting the rights of the other people we encounter in that environment. I believe that maintaining our obligation to show civility toward others in shared spaces is very important—perhaps more so now than ever before.

In order for any of us to truly feel "at home," there needs to be a space of safe public interaction that we can all pass through *on our way* home. We each need to be able to enjoy this special space without feeling threatened or out of place. This respect for shared space is central to one of the basic institutions of human society: The neighborhood.

It's all too common for the areas that *used* to be known as neighborhoods to be undermined or rendered completely dysfunctional. One of the big reasons for this is that the people who occupy shared spaces in these areas treat these spaces as their own private property, but they are not. Everyone who shows up in a shared space needs to understand that it *is* shared space—and resolve to respect the rights of others. When that doesn't happen, people don't feel safe outside of their own homes, and a kind of siege mentality can set in. That means more polarization, more disrespect, and more dysfunction. It's a negative cycle. And gentlepeople have a duty to try to turn it around.

Respecting your rights in the shared space that you and I occupy together means that I don't talk so loudly that you can't focus on what you want to focus on. (Think of how often people speak out loud during movies now, completely disregarding the rights of others to enjoy the film.) It means I don't have loud telephone conversations on the bus or subway. (Haven't you been on the receiving end of this kind of disrespect in a shared space? I know I have.) It means I don't litter, and it means I clean up after my dog if I've used the shared space to take that dog for a walk. (Many of our city streets are foul and unhealthy because some people refuse to extend even minimal common courtesy to other people who will be using the space.)

These aren't small issues. They have a *huge* cumulative impact. When shared spaces aren't respected, the people who pass through those spaces are less likely to treat each other with civility—and less likely to make adjustments for points of view and goals that conflict with their own. People who refuse to respect the rights of others in public parks, subways, and theaters aren't likely to show much respect for the rights of others anywhere else! In a very real sense, the viability of our society as a whole depends on our ability to behave as gentlepeople in our shared spaces—and to respond appropriately, politely, and tactfully when others fail to do the same.

> ## WHAT DOES IT LOOK LIKE?
> What's one way that you could spread goodwill and decency in a shared space that you find yourself in regularly? What would happen if you took action to do so?

CHAPTER TEN

Don't Use Profanity: Even if Others Do.

"Profanity is the effort of a feeble brain to express itself forcibly."

—Spencer W. Kimball

It almost seems impossible to believe now, but it's true. There really was a time when the vast majority of celebrities and public figures—actors, politicians, comedians, athletes, you name it—carefully avoided using even the mildest curse words whenever they knew that the public could hear what they were saying.

The Gentle Life

It's true. Nobody uttered swear words. Nobody relied on being bleeped out—or went out of their way to use rough language when they knew it couldn't get bleeped out. No hit songs had "explicit" tags or needed them. Even mainstream comedians, screenwriters, and storytellers who fell into the now-obsolete category of "risqué" used only inference; they never made direct, explicit sexual references while the cameras were rolling or the microphone was live. That was just the way society operated. By the way, back then, "risqué" meant simply that grownups could put two and two together if they wanted to, but the kids wouldn't even know that anything serious had been said or depicted. The essence of risqué, back in the day, was a situation like the following: In the classic film *Casablanca,* after Humphrey Bogart and Ingrid Bergman kiss, the camera cuts away to an exterior shot, and then returns to the same room, some time later. Left unexplored was the question of how the two characters spent that time together. Maybe they kept on kissing … or maybe things got more serious. We didn't know. The filmmakers let us figure that one out on our own. We didn't have to see everything laid out in lurid detail, and we didn't have to hear the main characters talking in an explicit fashion to know that they were in love. And you know what? The movie was better for it. The ambiguity and the uncertainty and the tension were more thoughtful and engaging than one of today's predictable explicit sex scenes would have been.

That all seems like a very, very long time ago. Some might say it was a time of innocence. I feel more like saying that it was a time of responsibility. There were certain lines people simply didn't cross in public, partly because they knew it was possible, and indeed likely, that children were watching and listening.

This wasn't "censorship." It wasn't an assault on anyone's freedom of speech. It was how we agreed to conduct ourselves as a culture. And I think it was a good agreement back then, and it's a good agreement right now. Specifically, I think it's worthwhile to live up to the standard of behavior observed by gentlepeople by making and keeping an agreement not to publicly use profanity—or words and phrases meant to stand in for profanity as coded messages. Why is that agreement worth making and keeping with ourselves? Because brutal, coarse, and uncivil language has the power to degrade human discourse— and we don't want to live in a society where that is the default setting. All too often now, we turn on the television or watch a YouTube video or listen to a hit song, and it seems that one of the specific goals of the artist must be to drag people down with vicious and unwholesome words rather than lift them up. But I believe gentlepeople know that the words we choose matter.

If you agree that words matter, let me challenge you to

raise the standard through a personal commitment: Don't use profanity (or sound-alike code words) in public places. Even if the people around you fail to live up to this standard—*especially* if the people around you fail to live up to this standard—start thinking more carefully about what comes out of your mouth!

A great yardstick to consider using here is the "tattoo test." If you wouldn't want a word or sentence to be tattooed on your forehead, then don't say it publicly! Adhering to this test will help to eliminate not only profanity, but all kinds of unfortunate, instantly regrettable speech from your public discourse. Your life will be better for it.

WHAT DOES IT LOOK LIKE?

What might you lose if you stopped using profanity altogether? What might you gain?

CHAPTER ELEVEN

If You Drink, Drink in Moderation: Respect the Environment That You Share With Others.

"O God, that men should put an enemy in their mouths to steal away their brains!"

—**WILLIAM SHAKESPEARE** *(Othello, Act II, Scene iii)*

When used responsibly, alcohol can be a good thing, but too often, the risks clearly outweigh the potential benefits.

The Gentle Life

Gentlepeople know that drinking to excess is a mistake, and they know how to stop themselves well short of making that mistake. They understand that dealing with a drunk is no one's idea of a good time, and they realize that the feelings of others really do matter when it comes to deciding what is acceptable behavior and what isn't.

For many people, maintaining appropriate boundaries when it comes to alcohol consumption is not much of a struggle. If we're out at a social gathering, and we know someone else is doing the driving so that we can get home safely, we know that one or two drinks is a viable standard, and we don't have trouble finding the right balance for ourselves. I know that I had to work for a while to find that balance. The truth is that I drank too much as a teenager, and I found myself flirting with disaster, including jail time and dying young—consequences that some of the other teenagers I got into trouble with sadly experienced. I was one of the lucky ones. After coming to understand the destructive potential of alcohol, I gave up excessive drinking.

But let's be frank here: There are some people for whom even a little alcohol is not a good idea. If you're a gentleperson, that means you've got to have the strength of character to recognize when that person is you. If you fall into that category, it's time to make a decision: Are you going to change your way of living? It's not always easy to make that kind of decision. It's not always fun. And you may not be able to do it alone. But sometimes saying goodbye to something you've grown used to is necessary. If such a step is warranted in your case, you may want to consider writing a goodbye letter to alcohol.

Here's an example of what such a letter might look like. Please feel free to customize it as you see fit.

Dear Alcohol –

When we met when I was just a young man, and I had no idea how huge a role you would eventually play in my life. I thought you were a wonderful friend—always available, always ready to help me relax, always eager to help me connect with others. But before long I realized there was another side to our relationship. Where I thought there was availability, Alcohol, there was really your jealous possessiveness—you literally didn't want anyone else in my life. Where I thought there was relaxation, there always came tension and conflict. Where I thought there was connection with other people, there was always damage and betrayal. But I realized all this too late. I came to rely on you too much, and I eventually reached the point where I literally couldn't get through the day without you. Now I can see what kind of "friend" you really are. You've sabotaged my relationships with everyone else, ransacked my memory, undermined my ability to make a living, and stolen so many days from my calendar—days either spent with you or recovering from being in your company—that I can't even begin to estimate how much time I've lost. You've turned me into someone I don't want to be. You've distanced me from my family. You've made me look at least ten years older than I really am. You've threatened my health. And if I continue to spend any of my time with you, you're going to drive me to an early grave. For these reasons, Alcohol, I've decided that it simply isn't healthy for me to continue my friendship with you. I'm drawing the line. I don't want to be with you anymore. You've got a lot of charisma, and it's been an interesting stretch of time, but I realize now that you just aren't good for me. Please keep your distance. We are done. Sincerely, (NAME).

If you find that you can't make your "goodbye" message stick, you may want to consider acknowledging that reality as a sign that it's time for you to start looking for some help. There is no shame in that—the only shame would be in failing to acknowledge the reality of your situation, and that's something gentlepeople don't do.

If you're looking for help in getting past an alcohol or substance abuse problem, please consider calling Alcoholics Anonymous, Narcotics Anonymous, or a similar support group so you can chart a new way forward in your life.

If You Drink, Drink in Moderation

WHAT DOES IT LOOK LIKE?

Which approach to alcohol makes the most sense for you—moderation or abstinence? What specific actions do you need to take based on what you're observing about the impact of alcohol on your most treasured relationships?

CHAPTER TWELVE

Be Faithful to Your Loved Ones: Including, but not Limited to, Your Spouse.

"We have to recognize that there cannot be relationships unless there is commitment, unless there is loyalty, unless there is love, patience, persistence."

—**Cornel West**

Gentlepeople keep their commitments.
This principle applies to short-term commitments, like what you're going to do on a project that you take

on at work—and how you're going to update the people who are collaborating with you about how you're progressing on that project.

It also applies to long-term commitments. I mean those commitments that involve our loved ones—which I believe are the commitments that truly define us as people. These are the commitments that matter. If you've made a commitment to be a good spouse to someone, and you're a gentleperson, you stick by that commitment, even when times are tough. If you've made a commitment to be a good parent, and you're a gentleperson, you stick by that commitment, even though parenting is probably the most difficult job in the world. Keeping those long-term commitments has a label that has fallen out of fashion in recent years: Being faithful. I believe that gentlepeople aren't afraid of that old-fashioned-sounding expression "being faithful." I believe they're committed to keeping faith in their relationships with those people who truly matter most in their lives. And I believe that commitment is part of their commitment to keeping faith with their Creator.

Of course there are conflicts and challenges in any marriage. Of course being a parent is going to mean that you have good days and bad days. And of course there are going to be times when there seem to be more reasons to walk away from a commitment than there are to follow through on it. Even so, I believe gentlepeople look for ways to keep their commitments, large and small, and I believe that they never stop looking. They never give up.

Very often, the failure to follow through on a long-term commitment to a spouse has its roots in what I call the "soulmate delusion." People come to believe that they are meant to be perfectly matched up with someone—and that this perfect match with the so-called "soulmate" means that times are going to be relatively easy most of the time. True commitment, I believe, demonstrates just the opposite about long-term relationships.

Long-term relationships, if they are to endure, take work. They take patience. They take a willingness to overlook the faults of another human being, secure in the knowledge that you have faults of your own that need overlooking. If we imagine that we've found a soulmate at the beginning of a relationship simply because of an easy connection or a quick sense of attraction, we're bound to be disappointed!

There is an art to keeping one's commitments to the most important people in one's life. I realize that mastery of that art does not come easily to everyone. In our period in history, about half of all marriages are now expected to disintegrate, splitting up countless millions of families. I know we live in hard times for families. But I am brave enough to suggest that gentlepeople are those who are willing to stop and think for a while before they take on a serious commitment—and willing to stop and think again, for a very long time indeed, before they walk away from one.

Gentlepeople recognize that a long-term commitment is sacred. And they recognize that it is up to each of us how sacred our commitments are, not just on the day we make them, but in the hard work of daily life that follows.

WHAT DOES IT LOOK LIKE?

Are you in survival mode in one of your most important relationships? Perhaps you can't even remember the last time you had fun with someone you're committed to. What would happen if you simply and straightforwardly expressed your concern to them—and reaffirmed your commitment to stand by them through thick and thin?

CHAPTER THIRTEEN

Dress Modestly: Modesty Is Always in Fashion.

"Nothing can atone for the lack of modesty; without which beauty is ungraceful and wit detestable."

—RICHARD STEELE

We live in an era in which skimpier and skimpier clothing trends and aggressively sexual marketing techniques have changed the way men and women—and particularly young men and women—define "normal" standards for public attire. People who push back against this trend are regarded as old-fashioned, or, even worse, as oppressive. I don't think it's oppressive to point out that a society that encourages teenage girls to walk around in clothes that conceal very little (or nothing at all) is doing those young women, and society as a whole, more harm than good. When we stop to consider how much of what people pay to wear in public is deliberately ripped, tightly form-fitting, askew, or simply cut open for the purposes of more aggressive display, it's hard not to conclude that we now live in an era in which human dignity has been placed on the auction block. Gentlepeople understand that young people are suffering as a result.

Gentlepeople also understand that modest clothing choices matter, and they try to serve as responsible role models in that regard. It doesn't stop there. They understand that the most popular choices when it comes to selecting one's attire, which are increasingly the clothing choices presented as normal in our hypersexualized media feeds, are not necessarily the choices that are in the best interests of families—and specifically not in the best interests of girls and young women.

Let's face it. We live in a time when the mass media's impact on young people—via computers, televisions, and smartphones—has never been higher, a time when standards of dress have never been more lurid, and a time when body image issues have never been more rampant. And yet role model after role model, celebrity after celebrity, adopts a standard of dress that would have been considered totally unacceptable just a few years ago. Doesn't that kind of "fashion sense" put pressure on kids to follow along? To pick clothes that are strategically ripped, trimmed, and minimized so as to draw attention to the youngster's body? And who does that help out ... besides the fashion industry?

Here is the reality with which we find ourselves confronted. When our kids see an unending stream of starlets, singers, and reality TV stars (male and female) prancing in front of the cameras wearing nearly nothing, they think that's normal. It's not. It's unhealthy, both on the level of the society and the level of the individual. And if you don't agree, consider the following sobering statistics:

- Fifty-two percent of today's teens report feeling that the media pressures them to change their body image to look more like media figures and people in advertisements.
- Forty-four percent of teens skip meals as a tactic for losing or controlling weight.
- Seventy-three percent of teens feel their appearance affects their personal body image.
- Fifty-six percent of teens feel that the media's advertisements are the main cause of their low self-esteem.

The Gentle Life

- Sixty-five percent of teens are afraid of gaining weight.
- Thirty-one percent of teens have at least one body part on which they would like to get surgery.

(Source: www.stageoflife.com,
"Statistics on High School Students and Teenagers")

That last trend is particularly disturbing. In recent years, there has been a dramatic rise in the number of teenagers seeking surgery to change how their bodies look. How is that a positive development? Is it even possible to look at a trend like that without wondering whether popular culture in general, and popular fashion in particular, has gone just a little too far in recent years?

I believe that grownups—people of character, gentlepeople—have an obligation to notice these trends, to connect the dots, and to set a good example. How a family member or a respected family friend dresses should matter *more* to our young people than how some movie star, fictional character, or game-show contestant dresses. If you are willing to be such a person of character, I ask you not only to make appropriate, modest choices in your own attire, but to support a young person in your world who needs encouragement and reinforcement to do the same.

Dress Modestly

WHAT DOES IT LOOK LIKE?

Do you know a young person who may have been caught up in the tide of immodesty—who may be feeling tremendous pressure to measure up to their peers? How could you talk through these issues in a way that is simple, non-judgmental, and holds out the promise of a better way?

CHAPTER FOURTEEN

Don't Use a Sporting Event as an Excuse to Abuse Others: Don't Scream, Swear, or Berate Others.

"Behavior is the mirror in which everyone shows their image."

—**Johann Wolfgang von Goethe**

There's something about public sporting events that seems to bring out the worst in some people. Who can say for sure why that is? It's a mystery to me. Whatever

THE GENTLE LIFE

is causing this, the problem seems to be accelerating as a prominent, impossible-to-miss symptom of a generalized loss of civility in society.

There are two very different scenarios for the kind of behavior I'm talking about.

The first is at professional sporting events—the events with teams that people pay money to see. Gentlepeople know full well that leaving mounds of garbage in the aisles or near their seats during these events is a form of behavior that they would never indulge in at home—so they don't indulge in it at the ballpark or stadium either. In addition, they don't drink too much alcohol. They don't swear at the top of their lungs at players or officials, even if they're unhappy about something that has happened on the field. They don't throw any object onto the field of play as a means of expressing their displeasure with someone's performance. And they certainly don't behave aggressively or boorishly toward children who happen to be nearby. Recently I saw a video of a very large adult fan reaching over to tear a baseball out of the tiny hands of a much younger fan, about eight years of age, who had just caught it! You see something like that and you start wondering about where our priorities are as grownups—and about how many grownups there really are out there.

In short, gentlepeople never, ever use the enjoyable act of rooting for a favorite team as an excuse for aggressive,

Don't Use a Sporting Event as an Excuse to Abuse Others

rude, irresponsible, and/or downright dangerous behavior. Unfortunately, gentlepeople appear to represent a shrinking minority of paying customers at professional baseball, football, basketball, and hockey contests, as each of these sports has plenty of examples of such uncivil displays on the part of the paying customers.

The other scenario, of course, is amateur events, and particularly those where children under the age of eighteen are the competitors. Let's begin with the question of the kind of example adults set at these games. A gentleperson knows how important it is to show unmistakable respect for people in authority at these contests, even if—or especially if—that official makes a decision that he or she doesn't like. I've seen too many games where parents were howling at the top of their lungs about the inadequacies of the official who was in charge of interpreting the rules, making decisions about events on the field, and keeping the game moving forward smoothly. What kind of message does a parent who routinely abuses and disrespects officials send to the kids in the stands and on the field? A toxic one! "Intimidate others, and the breaks will start going your way." Is that really the kind of society we want to live in?

I wish that all-too-common offense brought us to the end of the list of assaults on decency at amateur sporting events, but unfortunately it doesn't. There's one more example of boorish behavior I must share with you. I'm talking about the countless parents who can be heard shouting at their kids at these events—and I don't mean shouts of encouragement!

These are shouts that tell the athlete on the field, in no uncertain terms, that he or she failed to live up to the high standards of the parent. They also tell the child that the parent in question is willing to make a public scene over the perceived failure, over and over again. Talk about a recipe for destroying someone's self-esteem! Consistently sending a debilitating message along the lines of "You aren't good enough" in private is foolish and dangerous enough—but what on earth possesses some parents to constantly humiliate their children *in public* in this way? I simply cannot understand that. A gentleperson never, ever puts undue pressure on a young person to perform on the field—and certainly never humiliates a young athlete in public.

Furthermore, gentlepeople understand the vulnerability that many young people feel as they engage their peers in competition. This is why they need to make sure that their words and actions communicate their rock-solid approval.

Don't Use a Sporting Event as an Excuse to Abuse Others

WHAT DOES IT LOOK LIKE?

What message are you sending through your behavior as a spectator at sporting events—whether those of professional athletes or people you know personally? What message would you like to send?

CHAPTER FIFTEEN

Choose Better Entertainment Than the Crowd Does: The Fact That a Movie, Song, or TV Show Is Popular Does not Mean It's Right for You.

"Americans appreciate bad taste. If they didn't, America wouldn't look the way America does."

—P.J. O'Rourke

The Gentle Life

Over the last twenty years or so, there has been a profusion of cultural emptiness in our popular entertainment.

When I say "emptiness," I don't just mean "entertainment I don't like." There's lots of entertainment I don't prefer that doesn't qualify as emptiness. I mean entertainment that aims low and hits its target. If the entertainment in question is predicated on making a real, live person (not a character played by an actor) feel shame or embarrassment ... if the entertainment in question is explicitly pornographic ... if the entertainment in question results in a real person subjecting himself or herself to physical or psychological trauma in order to score lots of views online ... then I submit that the entertainment in question is empty—and that gentlepeople shouldn't watch it, no matter how popular it may become.

Using the three-part definition of cultural emptiness that I've just shared with you, it's hard not to conclude that a lot of money is being made these days by selling empty entertainment to people. That's a failure of industries, a failure of families, and a failure of society as a whole. The herd mentality is not serving us well. We are drinking deeply from places we should be avoiding, and I believe gentlepeople have a moral obligation to make better choices and set a better example. If you're reading these words, I

Choose Better Entertainment Than the Crowd Does

believe you can use your purchasing power to create those better choices and live that better example. And I hope you will.

There really is such a thing as "good taste." Much of the entertainment that's out there exhibits good taste. But not all of it. Some of it is empty, as I've defined it. There was a time when voyeurism, pornography, and total self-obsession really were regarded as off limits in the realm of popular entertainment. I believe there still are such standards as "good taste" and "bad taste." I believe we don't have to entertain ourselves with emptiness. I believe gentlepeople know the difference between those two ways of passing the time. They know that pornography is in bad taste, even when it's dressed up and given good lighting. They know that garbage is in bad taste, even when it's delivered or authorized by someone who's very famous. And they know that TV shows that document the very worst of human nature and call it "reality" are in bad taste—even if the ratings are good. Put simply, gentlepeople don't assume that a piece of culturally empty entertainment is worth watching or listening to, just because lots of other people are watching or listening to it.

If you agree with me, please make your home a better place when it comes to entertainment!

The Gentle Life

WHAT DOES IT LOOK LIKE?

Have you selected forms of entertainment that show people engaging in behaviors that wouldn't be acceptable in your own life or home? Why or why not? Do you need to make any changes based on what you're observing right now?

CHAPTER SIXTEEN

Make Dinnertime a Sacred Event for Your Family: Give Each Other Your Undivided Attention During This Special Time.

"The shared meal is no small thing. It is a foundation of family life, the place where our children learn the art of conversation and acquire the habits of civilization: Sharing, listening, taking turns, navigating differences, arguing without offending."

—MICHAEL POLLAN

The Gentle Life

Please don't be frightened by the word "sacred." Feel free to think of dinnertime as simply being "off limits" to anything other than the members of the family who are gathered around the table. My point here is not that gentlepeople follow any specific religious practice—I know they are a diverse bunch—but rather that they make a habit of giving their families priority at least once a day, at the main meal. And that is as it should be.

I do consider dinnertime sacred, as a time for gratitude and communion as a family, and I know I'm not alone in that. But whether or not you choose to say a prayer before eating, as we do in my family, I know you will want to follow the lead of gentlepeople and wholesome families everywhere by making sure dinnertime is uninterrupted family time, not just once in a while, but as a matter of settled habit. That means turning off the television, turning off the phones, and turning off the computer. It's possible that the younger people in your household will need a little loving support as you do this shutting-off routine together. Give them that love and support. Make turning off the technology part of your family ritual. This may take a little practice and a little persistence. But it is worth it.

Multiple studies have linked a committed family routine of regularly sharing dinners together with countless benefits for the younger members of the family, including lower levels of

Make Dinnertime a Sacred Event for Your Family

illicit sexual activity, eating disorders, tobacco use, marijuana use, violence, depression, binge drinking, and suicidal thoughts. One group of researchers even found that kids who came from families that shared the dinner hour together were better at bouncing back from episodes of online bullying than kids whose families never ate together or only rarely did so.

Still other studies have shown that children who regularly eat dinner with their parents experience less stress in life, have a more positive outlook on the future, and are more likely to communicate well with their parents. So why on earth don't more parents make this kind of family-centered meal a priority?

There's one simple answer: Television.

As a society, we have gotten used to the habit of watching TV while we eat. This is a real shame, because virtually all of the documented benefits I've just shared with you about family mealtime disappear when families switch on the television at dinnertime. Not only do benefits disappear—studies have also shown that there is a distinct negative impact. Kids who get into the habit of watching television during dinnertime are more likely to be obese than kids who don't. Obesity, of course, carries with it a whole host of related health and well-being problems.

The bottom line here is a simple one. Families used to make the dinner hour something special and uninterruptible. Now, on the whole, they don't. In fact, many adolescents take their dinner plates into their bedrooms and shut the door so they can eat alone! That's a downward spiral, and it needs to change. Our lives will be better off, our families will be better off, and our societies will be better off, if we go back to the uplifting standard of sharing focused, caring, technology-free communication with our loved ones at meal time.

Once you've turned off all of your devices and gathered around the table, what will you do to connect with one another while you eat? I think the best thing is to cultivate gratitude. One of my favorite ways to do that is a practice that my wife and I have engaged in for quite some time: Keeping—and sharing—a gratitude journal. After eating or before bedtime, Carol and I each share three or more things that we experienced that day that we are grateful for—and we record them in our gratitude journals.

As human beings, we too often gravitate toward complaining, grumbling, gossiping, and other less-than-ideal behaviors with one another. This is why it's important to keep a gratitude journal—to make sure that you're not overlooking the many joys and benefits of life. The meal is the perfect place to share your entries for the day.

My experience suggests that once you've gotten into the habit of celebrating the good things in one another's lives, you'll never look back!

WHAT DOES IT LOOK LIKE?

What would happen if everyone in your home put away their phones and turned off the television during meal time?

CHAPTER SEVENTEEN

Be Humble: Don't Boast or Brag.

*"Perhaps the less we have,
the more we are required to brag."*

—**John Steinbeck**, in *East of Eden*

Gentlepeople don't put on airs.
That means they don't engage in self-focused, self-obsessed, self-aggrandizing talk. They don't go out of their way to win attention for the things they have done, and they certainly don't go out of their way to grab credit for things they *haven't* done. They don't begin every other sentence with

the words "I" or "my." They don't believe that every conversation in which they take part has to revolve around their accomplishments, experiences, or future plans. And they don't imagine for a moment that the real point of any social gathering is for them to be worshiped, revered, or flattered.

Gentlepeople believe (to use a time-worn phrase) that their actions will always speak louder than their words. And that means they never, ever boast or brag.

One of the strangest and saddest trends in popular culture—for me at any rate—is the vast profusion of boasting and bragging in contemporary music and entertainment. You can't go anywhere these days without hearing some rap star singing some surrealistically self-absorbed love song to himself and his possessions, or without seeing some self-obsessed reality television star holding forth about her own magnificence and importance. It's as though these people only feel they exist if they are making the case for their superiority to someone else. It all comes off as rather shallow and insecure—which is, I think, exactly the opposite effect from the one intended—and it makes one feel more than a little concerned for the millions of people who consider these celebrities to be role models. Do they really believe that shouting their own praises to the heavens is the way to win anyone over? To accomplish anything worthwhile? To create a meaningful bond with another human being?

Be Humble

Here's an interesting challenge for you: Try to think of a single prominent current celebrity whose primary trait is humility. I'm not talking about someone who gets a lot of good press for charitable work—I'm talking about someone whose primary aim in life is to put others first and put oneself second. Such figures don't command a lot of attention from the media.

We simply don't celebrate humble people on a global scale. I believe that means we need to do more to celebrate them in our families, our neighborhoods, and our communities. If you're committed to being a gentleperson, I submit that you should be committed to serving as a role model for humility to the important people in your life ... and that you should make a point of not participating in the "I boast, therefore I am" cult so popular in our newsrooms, our politics, and our social media. Avoid that cult! Follow the example of gentlepeople by letting your actions speak louder than your words, and bear in mind the possibility that (as Ernest Hemingway once observed) true nobility lies, not in being superior to someone else, but in being superior to your former self.

WHAT DOES IT LOOK LIKE?

Do the celebrities you talk about most in your home exhibit pride or humility? Does your speech gravitate toward discussion of your own accomplishments? How could you champion humility in your personal conduct and in your entertainment choices? What impact would doing so have on the people you care for most?

CHAPTER EIGHTEEN

Know When to Forgive Others: Even if They Don't Ask!

"Forgiveness is an act of the will, and the will can function regardless of the temperature of the heart."

—**Corrie ten Boom**

Gentlepeople are eager to identify and seize opportunities to forgive others, partly because they have come to understand their own daily need for forgiveness. Of course, this is part of following the Golden Rule, which we considered in an earlier chapter. It's perhaps the most important extension of that rule, since all of us who are honest with ourselves know that we need forgiveness for the mistakes that we have made in our own lives, and therefore should be willing to extend forgiveness to others.

There is a fascinating and common misconception about forgiveness that I think we should examine here. Many people believe that in order to forgive someone, the individual we are considering forgiving has to be deeply repentant—and we must believe that the problem that arose in the past is unlikely to arise again. This is not how the great spiritual teachers of history approached forgiveness. Most of them took a much more radical approach, the approach of forgiving someone who may not even have realized that there was any need for forgiveness.

Although it's good to be able to get to the point of reconciliation with someone whom we feel has wronged us, it's not essential in order for true forgiveness to take place. All true forgiveness really means is that we let go of our right to be angry about a past action, based first and foremost on our compassion for the other person as a fellow human being. This is the ultimate in gentle behavior, in my view. And here's a surprise: It's something we need to do for our own benefit.

True forgiveness really is a gift—and not only to the one being forgiven. It allows the one forgiving to move on, to stop letting some unfortunate event in the past define who we are in the present or who we will be in the future. It's all about realizing that the situation that hurt us or victimized us is over, and that no matter what happens from this point forward, we don't have to wake up each morning imprisoned by anything that happened in the past. So, we can choose to forgive whether or not we see repentance on the other side.

Don't get me wrong. There are certainly going to be serious moments within our relationships with others when it makes sense to confirm that there is a change of heart and a change of perspective before you say to the other person, "I forgive you." But let's be realistic. Those crisis moments, those moments of deep betrayal, those moments when the viability or even the existence of the relationship itself is on the line, are few and far between. Most of our opportunities to exercise our "forgiveness muscle" involve a relatively minor problem in the grand scheme of things—and some involve grudges that shouldn't even have existed in the first place. If the person in question is someone who matters to you, it's worth thinking long and hard before you withhold your forgiveness about something that falls into the category of "I understand how this person made that mistake, because I have made similar mistakes myself."

If that's the kind of situation you're looking at—and it usually is—my advice is that you take the high road, the road that is always open to the gentleperson. Be the bigger person. Be the one who makes connection and reconciliation possible. Be the one who says, "Let's move on." Be the one who forgives, without even drawing attention to the choice to forgive.

Forgiveness is a lifelong journey. As you make that journey, considering carrying with you the example we find in the Bible of forgiving *and forgetting*: "He has removed our sins as far from us as the east is from the west" (Psalm 103:12). Too often, we don't do the forgetting part very well. Of course, you can't literally remove an offense that someone has committed against you from your memory, but you can make a principled choice about how you will respond whenever that incident flashes across your mind. Biblical forgetfulness is about choosing not to count someone's prior unfortunate choices and behaviors against them—to treat them as if those things never happened. It isn't easy, but it's the right thing to do if we want to see the miracle of reconciliation occur.

WHAT DOES IT LOOK LIKE?

Do you find yourself regularly referring to a specific way that someone wronged you in the past? Why do you think that is? Would it be possible for you never to mention it again? What would happen as a result?

CHAPTER NINETEEN

Know When to De-escalate a Conflict: Not Every Battle Is Worth Winning.

"Conflict cannot survive without your participation."

—WAYNE DYER

Even if you don't feel emotionally ready to forgive someone, you can create the possibility of dialogue, or at least a cooling-off period, when you find yourself in the middle of a conflict that you know isn't serving anyone.

The Gentle Life

Of course, there is a time and place for conflict, and I know plenty of gentlepeople who are perfectly capable of defending their position when the need arises to do so. The real challenge comes in knowing when it is better to walk away than it is to stand your ground. A good example from the world of cinema of someone who knows this difference would be Rhett Butler in *Gone with the Wind*. Do you remember the scene where Butler is challenged to a duel by a hot-tempered young man ... and tactfully withdraws from the situation rather than making a scene? We later learn that he did so not because he was a coward, but because he knew he would kill the young man in question!

We need a little more of this kind of foresight when it comes to conflict management, I think. Not every battle is worth fighting, and not every fight is worth winning. Our best instincts about de-escalation only emerge with experience, I suppose, but my interactions with gentlepeople over the years suggest to me that two important best practices can and should be summarized here on this important subject. Here they are:

- ***If you feel you are too emotionally involved—meaning that you ask yourself "How am I feeling about this?" and you realize you are not thinking clearly—then it is time to call time-out and de-escalate the conflict.*** If you're too emotional, you're likelier to say or do something that you'll regret, something that can't be undone. Giving someone a piece of your mind is not gentle behavior. If you feel you cannot move beyond such subjects as how you've been mistreated, what's fair and what isn't, or what you could or might do to retaliate, take a deep breath. Those topics are flashing red lights that you may need to take some time away from the person with whom you're in conflict.

- ***Similarly, if you don't feel you can bring about productive change by engaging in a conversation with someone, you should take a break and find a way to disengage.*** The only *good* reason to engage in conflict is that you are hoping to produce a positive outcome. If that's your intention, more power to you. But if you do a quick self-assessment and conclude that you're less interested in a win/win outcome than you are in scoring points at someone else's expense or getting the last word, then you should consider the possibility that you're not engaging as a gentleperson would. For your sake and the sake of the relationship, it's time to step away. Check back in when you are ready to work on a solution that will make sense to both sides.

Conflict is a fact of human life, whether it unfolds in the home, in the workplace, or anywhere else. Relationships in which there is zero conflict are unlikely to be meaningful or satisfactory to either side. We can't escape conflict, and it's a mistake to try. But gentlepeople know that the *quality* of the conflict—how the conflict is handled—is what really matters. Gentlepeople don't make *toxic* conflict a regular part of their lives. That means they engage fully when they engage—and they step away without hesitation, like Rhett Butler.

In order to step away from a conflict when you are too emotionally involved or not focused on a mutually beneficial outcome, do what gentlepeople do. Say something like this:

"I'm sorry—I really don't think I can have this conversation right now. I need to take a break. Can we pick this up again a little later?" By the way, if the person you're having the conflict with asks "When?" that's a good sign. Set a time and place when you can continue the discussion—and follow through.

You really do have a choice about whether or not to take part in an argument. If you sense the time isn't right, step away!

In the next chapter, we'll take a look at how gentlepeople handle themselves when it *is* time to pick up the conflict and manage it constructively.

Know When to De-escalate a Conflict

WHAT DOES IT LOOK LIKE?

Can you see yourself hitting the pause button in a heated discussion with someone you love? What would you say, and what would happen as a result?

CHAPTER TWENTY

Know When to Embrace Conflict: Use Constructive Conflict Management Strategies.

"Peace is not the absence of conflict. It is the ability to handle conflict by peaceful means."

—**Ronald Reagan**

In the previous chapter, I shared a few thoughts with you on the essential skill of de-escalating conflict by calling time-out and giving yourself and/or another person time to cool off. This is indeed a critical relationship skill, and it's one of the most important tools in the gentleperson's kit. But it's not the only relevant skill when it comes to conflict management, and over-reliance on it can cause serious problems. So in this chapter, I want to take a look at five equally essential strategies for *managing* conflicts that arise in a gentle fashion. All five of them are important to understand and practice, and each of the five must be used from time to time.

Accommodation: This means simply giving the other person what he or she wants. It's important to understand that this really is a conflict management strategy, and that it is indeed the right response in some situations. It's not the right answer *all* the time, of course, but it's a major mistake for us not to even consider yielding when we are in a conflict with someone. If the stakes are low and accommodating the other person will keep the peace, this option is worth considering. Gentlepeople know, however, that if this is the *only* conflict resolution strategy used, there are eventually going to be problems. There needs to be a healthy mix, for the simple reason that the stakes are not always low and giving in does not always keep the peace!

Avoidance: This means putting off the conflict indefinitely, in the hopes that the problem will be resolved without any further discussion. Although this may sound like a failure of leadership, it's really not—as long as the avoidance strategy is deployed judiciously. Some problems really do go away when you avoid them. Some situations really do resolve themselves. Just as with the accommodation strategy, however, it's important to recognize that this cannot be the *only* conflict resolution strategy you pursue, nor should it be relied on too heavily.

Collaboration: This means saying, "Let's work together to come up with a better solution here." A key to making the collaboration strategy work is being willing to drop, for the moment, our own perspective on the problem, and acknowledge that other people may have different perspectives on what is happening. Gentlepeople know how to send the message "I realize you have your own experience of this situation, and I want to hear what it is." That's an essential prerequisite to a grown-up conversation about what's not working in the current process—and how it could change for the better.

Compromise: This means saying, "I'll give you X if you give me Y." This strategy assumes that both sides can get closer to a position that's acceptable, but not ideal, by "horse-trading." As a practical matter, it really only works when both parties have roughly equivalent authority and bargaining powers. Because of this, you may want to use this one sparingly when you're resolving conflict with someone who reports to you in a business setting. Collaboration is usually better suited to situations where you're dealing with conflicts that involve employees than compromise is.

Competition: This means settling the disagreement by means of a contest or competition whose rules are well understood and accepted as fair ahead of time by all concerned. Although this can be an extremely effective strategy, it has the drawback of generating winners and losers, which can be a cause of resentment over time if one side loses consistently. Gentlepeople know that no one likes to lose all the time, so they use this conflict management tool sparingly, and they maintain a balanced approach that employs the other four strategies as well.

WHAT DOES IT LOOK LIKE?

Can you identify a recent conflict that went poorly for everyone involved? Which of the above strategies do you think might have allowed things to go better?

CHAPTER TWENTY-ONE

Be Kind to People Who Need Help: Be the One to Step Forward and Assist Them.

"No act of kindness, however small, is ever wasted."

—**Aesop**

This is one of those items that you wouldn't think anyone needed a lot of reminding about. But, alas, it turns out that we do. There is plenty of evidence to demonstrate

The Gentle Life

that an alarmingly large number of people have gotten into the habit of ignoring individuals who obviously need assistance.

If you doubt that, conduct a little experiment the next time you're using public transportation during rush hour. When an elderly or disabled person or a pregnant woman gets on, how many people make way for that individual? How many offer him or her a seat? How many make a point of asking whether the person needs help getting on or off the vehicle and volunteer their own assistance? It's embarrassing to me to see how often the people sitting right next to someone who needs a seat don't immediately get up. Sometimes those of us who are sitting far away have to get up, walk through the crowd, make the offer, and lead the person to a faraway empty seat!

The instinct to offer assistance to obviously vulnerable people is one of the things that holds society together. Expressing this instinct really ought to be something that comes naturally for all of us. After all, we or someone we love may be the ones who need a little extra consideration at some point in our lives! Unfortunately, even this consideration appears to be losing traction, and yet another vital connecting bond appears to be fraying. The actress Olivia Wilde recently called out New York subway riders for pretending that she either didn't need a seat or didn't exist during a very long ride. She was nine months pregnant. In an indignant Twitter post (and who could blame her for being indignant?) she wrote to the city's subway riding population at large, "I'll just stand riiiiight next to your head and pray I go into labor."

How many other pregnant women and elderly or disabled people have had similar experiences? Judging from the popularity of this topic online, it appears to be quite a few, all across the country! That's a sad state of affairs.

I'm not *just* talking about public transportation, of course. I'm talking about any situation where someone who is operating at a disadvantage needs a little additional help and consideration from an able-bodied individual. Gentlepeople are more than happy to give up their place in line to such a person, let him or her have the next cab, or let him or her go first on the elevator. They know that this helps more people than just the individual who's facing a physical challenge—it also helps everyone who is watching to understand from direct experience what it means to be a gentleperson.

Being kind to people we know need a little more time than we do, a little more space than we do, or a little more of our patience is the kind of behavior that really should be automatic for all of us. Until it is, make sure you're one of the people on the bus who sets the right example.

WHAT DOES IT LOOK LIKE?

When was the last time you noticed someone around you who could have used a bit of extra help or space? If it has been a while, why do you think that is? What could you do differently from now on, and what do you think would happen as a result?

CHAPTER TWENTY-TWO

Take Time to Pray: Communicate With Your Creator.

"Lord, make me an instrument of thy peace.
Where there is hatred, let me sow love,
Where there is injury, pardon;
Where there is doubt, faith;
Where there is despair, hope;
Where there is darkness, light;
And where there is sadness, joy.

O Divine Master, grant that I may not so much seek to be consoled as to console,

The Gentle Life

to be understood as to understand,
to be loved, as to love.

For it is in giving that we receive,
It is in pardoning that we are pardoned,
and it is in dying that we are born to eternal life."

—Francis of Assisi

I believe that gentlepeople take time out to commune with God through prayer.

Please don't be frightened away by the word "prayer." It simply means "time set aside for communication with your Creator." How you manage that communication is up to you.

Your prayer time might take the form of a private walk. It might have you on your knees, clasping your hands together, or it might entail silent meditation while sitting all alone in a room. It might not "look" like prayer at all to others around you—like on a trip to the ballpark, where thirty thousand other people are taking in the same event. But if you're using the time to talk to your Creator, it all matters. If the time is spent without distractions, and it gives you the opportunity to come closer to the source of all things, then that's time you've invested in prayer. And while it may not be popular to say this in all social circles, prayer is a basic human need that gentlepeople are careful not to overlook.

The kind of time I'm talking about could be ten or fifteen minutes, or it could be several hours. But if you're a gentleperson, I believe you're going find a way to take *some* time, at *some* point in your week, to connect with God. And I believe the intention that guides that prayer is what determines success or failure in this life. Our intention during prayer is what makes our purpose in life clear. That's what makes prayer an essential practice.

There's an interesting historical event involving prayer that has to do with a famous nautical disaster. Perhaps you've heard about it.

Back in April of 1912, there were three different ships that were each in a position to aid the wounded ship Titanic after it collided with an iceberg. The first ship was called the Sampson. That vessel was just seven miles away from the Titanic. Its crew members saw the Titanic's white flares signaling danger, but they had a problem. They had been hunting seals illegally and didn't want to have to make an accounting of their whereabouts to the authorities. So they turned and went in the opposite direction from the crippled ship. I think of this ship as representing people who are so absorbed in their own lives that they can't be bothered to think about what their real purpose in life is—people who say they have no time to pray or interest in doing so.

The Gentle Life

The second ship was called the Californian. This ship was all of 14 miles away from the Titanic. It was surrounded by huge fields of ice. When the Californian's captain, awakened by his crew, looked out from his window and saw the white flares, he knew that the ice that surrounded his ship meant a rescue mission would be dangerous. He opted to go back to bed. He would check the ice conditions in the morning and see whether it made sense to proceed. The Californian represents those people who know that God has given them a purpose in life and have identified what it is, but choose not to take action on it. They pretend not to know what they should do. These are people who pray, but don't make any attempt grow spiritually as a result of their prayer.

The third ship in a position to make a difference was called the Carpathia. This ship was the farthest away—58 miles from the scene of the collision with the iceberg. The Carpathia picked up the Titanic's distress signal over its radio. When the Carpathia's captain heard that message, he knelt down and asked God to make clear to him what he ought to do next. When he was done praying, he stood up, ordered that his ship turn around, and set a course straight through the ice fields, full steam ahead. This ship and its brave captain represent the people who use prayer to get clarity on their purpose in life—and then take action!

The Carpathia ended up rescuing 705 people from the

Take Time to Pray

wreckage of the Titanic. In the years following that now-famous rescue mission, the captain remarked more than once that he believed someone else's hands must have guided his ship's wheel through those dangerous fields of ice.

I think he was absolutely right.

> ## WHAT DOES IT LOOK LIKE?
>
> What do you think would happen if you took a few minutes to pray the next time you had a chance? Is there a specific plan that you want to make in light of what you've learned?

CHAPTER TWENTY-THREE

Commit to Lifelong Learning: It's a Journey That Never Ends.

"Self-education is, I firmly believe, the only kind of education there is."

—Isaac Asimov

There is a dangerous myth out there, one that we can either buy into or discard as we see fit. This myth is pervasive. So many people have accepted it as true that it's sometimes treated as though it were a fact. And so many

The Gentle Life

people are willing to accept it as a fact that our families, our organizations, and our country as a whole have suffered as a result.

The myth is this: *It's natural to stop learning and growing intellectually once you pass a certain age.*

You can make that "certain age" any number you want. Some people who propagate this myth place what I call the "mental death sentence" threshold at forty. Some put it at fifty. Some put it at sixty-five or seventy. But the truth is, wherever they put it, it becomes a tragic self-fulfilling prophecy. If you're a human being with a functioning brain—a brain that hasn't been dealt any unfortunate obstacles from problems such as birth defects, Alzheimer's disease, or physical injury—it is your birthright, and you have an important responsibility to yourself and others to keep learning and growing from the day you are born until the day you die. Gentlepeople know this.

Lots of other people, sad to say, don't.

Think of your own circle of connections, and you'll probably be able to quickly and easily come up with multiple examples of people who have made themselves prematurely old—and perhaps even prematurely dead—by closing themselves off to new information and new ideas. It's one of the tragedies of our era: People do this to themselves, and they do it by buying into the unfortunate myth that there is a time when they are supposed to stop being curious.

Speaking for myself, I know I've met plenty of people who seemed exhausted, cynical, and all but finished with life in their early to mid-forties—and I've also met plenty of people in their eighties, nineties, and beyond who were so alert, optimistic, vigorous, and engaged that they came across as being far younger than their chronological age. We each have the choice about which of those two groups we want to belong to. If we opt for the second group (and why on earth wouldn't we?!), then we have to adopt a simple principle, confirmed by modern science, about brain fitness: *Use it or lose it.*

Put simply, if we don't make a point of stretching our brains with new information—if we don't make a point of challenging our own assumptions and expanding our own skill sets—then our brain functioning, including our capacity to make new neural connections, begins to deteriorate. On the other hand, if we keep exercising our brains by doing things like learning new languages, visiting new places, or tackling problems that once seemed unsolvable to us, we will stay mentally younger, longer.

Another way to look at this reality is to accept that human beings were designed to encounter challenges at all ages ... and designed to adapt to those challenges. The moment we stop doing that—the moment we start sealing ourselves off from new

The Gentle Life

tasks, unfamiliar environments, and tricky puzzles—we accelerate the mental aging process. That's something that gentlepeople know doesn't serve them or the people they care about. So they commit to a course of lifelong learning! They never stop reading, exploring, discovering, and creating—no matter how many candles show up on the birthday cake. They refuse to retire! They may or may not keep working a full-time job, but they refuse to park themselves on the couch (or on the golf course for that matter), eliminate new stimuli, and begin the process of mental decay. They know the human brain is far too precious to misuse in that way!

Use it or lose it! To remind yourself of this vitally important principle, consider the following list of gentlepeople who kept learning, kept striving, and kept achieving, in many cases well beyond the so-called retirement age:

- Laura Ingalls Wilder began her career as a published author of the acclaimed *Little House on the Prairie* books in her mid-sixties.
- Benjamin Franklin signed the Declaration of Independence when he was 70 and pursued an active career as a scientist and diplomat in the years following that.
- Nelson Mandela became president of South Africa at age 76.

- Peter Mark Roget published his first thesaurus at the age of 73.
- Donald Trump became the President of the United States at age 70.
- I had the exhilarating experience of climbing a 14,500-foot mountain on my 70th birthday. As I completed the climb, I asked myself what I could do next—something audacious and over-the-top. The answer I landed on was to write a book—and you are now reading my eighth book!

Always be ready and willing to climb the next mountain!

WHAT DOES IT LOOK LIKE?

What's your "mountain"—that thing that even you can't quite imagine yourself doing? Will you embrace the challenge of scaling it? What's the next step, and when will you take it?!

CHAPTER TWENTY-FOUR

Disconnect Now and Then: Be Willing to Disengage From the Wired World.

"Find some quiet, private time. Allow yourself to slow down and relax. Find nature, meditate, or do nothing. Take a mental break. You'll gain the benefits of a quiet mind."

—Tom Giaquinto

The Gentle Life

I realize this chapter's advice will probably seem radical to some people who have grown used to the constant and often illusory sense of "connection" that modern communications technology offers us. Perhaps what I am advocating here will even seem extreme to those who are deeply accustomed to a constantly "connected" existence. But the personal example set by all the gentlepeople that it has been my privilege to know down through the years makes this guidance an imperative. None of those people—not one—has ever had the problem of being so locked into a given piece of communications technology that they consistently neglected the opportunity to give themselves some free time.

But what is free time? I can't answer that question without tipping my hat to one of my mentors, Dan Sullivan at Strategic Coach®, the leading company in entrepreneurial coaching. Dan taught me a concept that revolutionized, not just how I ran my business, but how I manage time each and every day. There are essentially three types of days in the time system that Dan taught me:

- **Focus days:** These are days when you're doing what you do best. You're highly engaged in a project that draws directly on your core competencies.
- **Free days:** These are days when you're doing whatever gives you the greatest sense of enjoyment and purpose

apart from your work. For many, it means spending uninterrupted time with their families. For others, it may mean a hobby that they find relaxing or exhilarating—or both!

- **Buffer days:** These are days when you're preparing for focus days or free days, mostly by developing new skills and delegating projects to others.

What I'm advocating for here is that you make sure you've built a reasonable amount of free time into your schedule. I'm talking about an extended period during which people can't text you, call you, e-mail you, or otherwise interrupt your privacy or your ability to be fully engaged with the people who matter most to you or the refreshing activity in progress. I mean time when you take conscious advantage of a decision to set aside at least 4-8 hours when you are not perpetually available to anyone and everyone who has your contact information. I mean time when you can slow down and hear yourself think.

Many people—too many, I think—simply no longer experience free time as I have defined it here.

When was the last time you did? That's not a rhetorical question. Please stop and think for just a moment about when the last time was when you literally *could not* have gotten a message from someone for several hours. (No, putting your phone on "do not disturb" mode while you sleep at night doesn't count.) Most of the people I talk to have to think long and hard ... and then tell me that they simply can't remember *any* time when that's been the case over the past six months.

That's too long to go without free time.

Gentlepeople know how important it is to step away once in a while from the constant barrage of communication that has almost come to define our lives in the modern world. They know that barrage is not how any of us should define our existences. We should all know better than that—which is why I really do want you to make the effort necessary to change your paradigm when it comes to taking a little time to yourself or with the people you love. That means putting down your phone. Getting away from your computer. Turning off the TV. Focusing on something or someone else.

What you do with this time is entirely up to you—as long as it doesn't involve interactive media. You can read a book. You can take a walk. You can clean the house. You can sit down in a nice spot in your backyard and do nothing at all if that's what helps you to feel like you've caught up with your private time. But the key is to do **something** that can't easily be interrupted by the outside world and that allows you to relax and refuel. I recommend you schedule 4-8 hours or more of free time at least once a week.

There are plenty of people who tell me that they're simply not cut out for this kind of uninterruptible private time, that they don't feel safe or comfortable taking an hour away from

Disconnect Now and Then

the wired, connected world. These are usually the same people who complain about experiencing too much stress in their lives and ask what can be done about that! Here's what I say to them: "Once upon a time, believe it or not, people went for days, weeks, or even months at a time without being able to be certain they'd heard the latest news and gossip or read the latest headlines. Experiencing several hours or more of free time per week wasn't a crisis then, and it doesn't have to be a crisis now. If there's an emergency, you'll find out about it soon enough from one of your friends who has a functioning telephone and a means of getting your attention. In the meantime, don't assume you can't do this. Assume you can—and see what happens!"

WHAT DOES IT LOOK LIKE?

What would happen if you set aside 4-8 hours during the next week to disconnect and do something that refreshes you, without any possibility of being interrupted? Would you need to tell anyone about your plans? Will you schedule such a time right now?

CHAPTER TWENTY-FIVE

Seek, Find, and Keep a Role Model: Be Aspirational!

"If we want to do more than just drift along in the cultural stream, it helps to search out models of goodness, purity, honor, character, and courage, both in our entertainment and in real life ... The great advantage to having such heroes is that they don't badger us into changing; they inspire us to want to change."

—**MICHAEL W. SMITH**

The Gentle Life

I have noticed that gentlepeople tend to be big believers in aspiration.

Aspiration simply means the habit of trying to do, be, and contribute more than you are doing, being, and contributing right now. It means not being satisfied with your past. It means knowing you are and always will be a work in progress. It means never imagining that you are finished while you are still above ground. It means setting your life's course in the direction of the person you could be, not the person you used to be.

Aspirational living is especially important for those who are of an advanced age. Life does not stop at age 60 or 65—the later years just may be your very best aspirational years!

Gentlepeople know that one of the most important strategies for living an aspirational life is to find someone from history who can call them forward and serve as a great role model ... and then figure out how *that* person managed to do better, be better and contribute more. They know that many of the same insights and strategies the role model used can be directly taken on or adapted by later generations.

Gentlepeople know how important it is to find someone you respect—someone who lived the kind of transformational life you want to live and made the kinds of contributions you want to make—and then ask yourself, "Okay, how did they do that?" The answers to that question shorten your learning curve. They

Seek, Find, and Keep a Role Model

show you where the joy and excitement and adventure of an aspirational life lie waiting for you to discover them.

Gentlepeople, in short, choose great role models on purpose, with the aim of living a certain kind of life, and they choose those role models wisely.

Most people *don't* choose their role models purposefully, consciously or wisely. Instead, they accept whatever default role model manages to pop up on the surface of the tide of random noise that we call pop culture.

I think this state of affairs is worth considering closely.

Notice what pop culture has done to us in recent years. Notice that the people we spend time with influence both our values and our aspirations. Our society has recently entered a phase where the majority of the people who live in it are presented (via television, movies, and the Internet) with any number of famous "friends." These are people whom millions of strangers now think of as social companions ... but who don't actually exist as friends in those people's lives. Sixty years ago, millions of people were *interested* in Marilyn Monroe. Today, millions of people imagine they *know* Kim Kardashian.

It's true. Lots of us really do come to think we know these people intimately, because we find ourselves engrossed in the fictional or not-so-fictional narratives they circulate. After all, we can gather lots of details about what we imagine their "real lives" are like from social media. And we come to think of them as "friends" and even "heroes." But the truth is, we *don't* know them intimately. And if we delude ourselves into believing that we know a supermodel, a singer, a rap star, a movie actor, or even a totally fictional superhero well enough to make that person our primary role model in life ... well, something has gone wrong somewhere along the line.

Regardless of how well we think we know them, our favorite celebrities are probably not the best role models for our lives. We should choose our role models with care ... rather than allowing pop culture to choose them for us.

Let me repeat that because the point is very important: I believe our role models *must* be chosen consciously. Some of our role models may well be family members or close friends who have made a big difference for us personally. Beyond that, though, I believe we should make sure our role models are people who inspired others by making a difference. They should be people who knew deep suffering or faced great challenges and responded constructively—in a way that benefited humanity as a whole. I'm talking about people like Jackie Robinson, who broke the color line in major league baseball when doing so meant facing death threats day after day (exemplifying the value of courage). I'm talking about people like Franklin D. Roosevelt, whose life and career were forever changed by polio, and who remade himself following that enormous personal tragedy and eventually led an entire nation through crisis after crisis (exemplifying the values of patriotism and resilience). I'm talking about people like Helen Keller, who made it past a debilitating childhood illness and overcame the twin handicaps of blindness and deafness to become a great writer and a world-renowned advocate for human possibility (exemplifying the values of perseverance and optimism).

These were great human beings, not because they were perfect—they weren't—but because they were aspirational.

In other words, they grew and learned over time. They knew they were works in progress. They made the most of their journey, even when the journey was difficult. They encountered obstacle after obstacle, adversity after adversity. They found ways to turn those obstacles into lessons ... and then turned those lessons into newer, better strategies for attaining their goals. As a result, they earned a place in our history books.

Now take a moment to consider the figures that the average Instagram user is most likely to look up to today as "heroes." What are their aspirations? What values do these people exemplify? Will anyone be writing history about any of them a century from now?

For the most part, these people are celebrities who are anything *but* aspirational in comparison with figures like Robinson,

The Gentle Life

Roosevelt, and Keller. What great obstacles have our biggest modern Internet celebrities overcome? A rap rival's insults? A temper tantrum from a fellow cast member on a reality show? A made-up alien attack they pretended to turn back in a movie? What have these people learned? What have they contributed? What have they given back to the rest of us? What are they aspiring to become, to achieve, to leave behind?

Typically, the answer is: Very little.

When I say that for the most part, today's "role models" are not aspirational in any meaningful sense, what I really mean is that they don't embody any comprehensible *values* beyond an obsession for personal success and a desire for extensive fame and wealth. Gentlepeople know that a truly aspirational life requires something far, far loftier than those aims ... and so they look to the history books, not to the television or social media feeds, to find the worthiest role models. And they learn everything they can.

They look for people whose lives were all about commitment and purpose—people who made a contribution. People who left the world a better place than they found it. And you know what? Because gentlepeople are likelier than others to read and learn about the role models who made a big difference, they live their lives with a distinct advantage.

Whenever they face a major challenge in their own lives,

Seek, Find, and Keep a Role Model

gentlepeople can ask themselves, "What would so-and-so have done?" And they can work out a meaningful answer—an aspirational answer, an answer that means something, not just to them, but to all the others in their world who are relying on them.

So if you happen to be facing a crisis, and you know that people are counting on you, and you're *still* not sure whether you'd rather ask yourself what Kendall Jenner would do in this situation or what Franklin Roosevelt would do, please read this chapter again from the beginning!

Please understand me. I'm not saying FDR should necessarily be your role model (although you could do a lot worse). But what I am saying is that you owe it to yourself to be sure to identify at least *one* truly great role model to guide your life whose example inspires you to dream big, learn big, and act big. I believe that this should be someone from history, someone you truly respect, someone who's worthy of the title of "role model." It should be someone you *want* to learn more about.

Do a little reading and find out all you possibly can about this person—and not just from one source. Read widely! Pick someone whose life is worthy of close study … and get a few different perspectives. Make it your aim to get to know the person as intimately as you can. Accept that, unlike an Internet sensation who may be here today and gone tomorrow, you could well be learning about your role model for years, or even decades—and enjoy that process!

Once you are on the path of learning about this person as a long-term pursuit, you can do what gentlepeople do. You can position yourself to make that individual's example, experiences, and insights the north point on your personal compass, and you can position yourself to live an equally aspirational life, knowing that you have a transformational role model.

> ## WHAT DOES IT LOOK LIKE?
>
> What would happen if you committed to learning about someone who made a great, positive impact—one that you would like to reproduce to some degree in your own life? Who is your transformational role model? Will you start learning right now?

CHAPTER TWENTY-SIX

Be a Role Model: Invest in Your Community, One Person at a Time.

"Example is leadership."

—**Albert Schweitzer**

In the previous chapter, I urged you to follow the example of gentlepeople down through the ages and look to history for a role model worthy of the name—someone you can learn about and learn from over time. In this chapter, I want to urge you to *become* a role model worthy of the name. Being a role model may sound intimidating to some, but it's really just another way of describing what it means to be a transformational friend—finding a specific individual you can mentor, coach, and support over time. Gentlepeople, in my experience, make a point of identifying at least one individual who will benefit from such a relationship. They change the world ... one person at a time.

The person whose transformation you champion could be a disadvantaged youth with whom you meet on a regular basis. You can relax, do something fun together, listen to his or her story, share your own story, talk about the art and skill of making the best life choices, and generally offer whatever help you can, whenever you can. Or you could serve as mentor to a new hire who works at your organization—perhaps someone just out of college who needs some guidance in the early phase of his or her career. By the same token, the person you befriend could be someone who is your age (or older!) who is trying to chart a new course in life in an area where you have significant experience. Whoever you choose to come alongside of, my advice is that you put the emphasis on developing a quality relationship with an individual who looks up to you. This should be a relationship in which you receive nothing in return—other than the satisfaction of watching someone grow, learn, and thrive thanks to your help.

Be a Role Model

The impact of a transformational friend can be incalculable—and even life-saving! I know this personally. You see, even though they passed away some time ago, for many decades I have benefited from the transformational influence of my older sister, Rose, and her husband, Gene. They took me in when I was stumbling down the path of life as a teenager and creating lots of heartache for everyone who cared about me. Without their grace in accepting me into their home despite my wild ways, I'm sure I would have wrecked my life.

Let's talk a bit more about what it means to be a transformational friend. Here's a few key aspects:

- ***Being a trusted advisor.*** In other words, being prepared to act in the other person's interests, not your own, and doing that consistently enough that the other person comes to trust you. The person you coach should never have any doubt about whose side you are on. He or she should trust you implicitly ... and look forward to hearing your insights before he or she makes any important decision.
- ***Being available and ready to listen whenever the other person faces a major challenge and really needs to talk.*** A major part of being a transformational friend is being ready, willing, and able to listen attentively, actively, and without prejudice. If the other person doesn't feel you've listened, the relationship will not be a productive one!

- ***Being in a position to help point the other person toward the resources he or she needs most.*** This could come in the form of practical help in getting clear on personal goals ... or training and skills development ... or introductions to other people who can help ... or even your own personal insights and experience on how the most worthwhile things end up getting done. Those are all resources that can make a difference.
- ***Being ready to offer your support in a way that is accessible and makes sense to the other person.*** You may love to talk about what you do best ... but this is not about you delivering a lecture for an hour straight. Instead, it's all about figuring out how the person you're helping learns best ... and then tailoring your approach to match up with his or her needs. If you're dealing with someone who's addicted to YouTube, for example, don't assume you should fight his or her viewing habits. That's swimming upstream! Be ready to swim with the current! Look for great, compelling, concise videos online that will help the person you're mentoring to get the information he or she needs, in a format that he or she can relate to easily.

A transformational friendship may last for years ... but remember that a single hour-long lunch meeting can have a huge impact. What matters more than the duration of the relationship

Be a Role Model

is your commitment to get to know the individual ... to understand his or her personality, life goals, and learning style ... and to share support and insights that will help him or her to grow and develop over time.

> *"Mentoring is a brain to pick, an ear to listen, and a push in the right direction."*
>
> — JOHN CROSBY

WHAT DOES IT LOOK LIKE?

Being a transformational friend seems like a big job, but like any other worthwhile choice, it's implemented one step at a time. Can you identify someone in your life who could benefit from your listening ear, experience, skills, or insight? What's the next step toward connecting with that person, and when will you take it?

NOTE: More information on how to be a transformational mentor can be found in the back of this book.

CHAPTER TWENTY-SEVEN

Give Financially to Charity: Offer Tangible Support to a Cause You Care About.

"When we give cheerfully and accept gratefully, everyone is blessed."

—MAYA ANGELOU

If you've made it this far in the book, I suppose it's going to come as no surprise to you that I'm advocating the gentle behavior of making a financial contribution to a charitable cause that means something to you personally. I think that particular behavior is in keeping with the spirit of everything I've shared with you thus far. Of course, there are plenty of ways to give other than financially, but let's put a hold on that subject for now. We'll look at other kinds of charitable giving in the next chapter. For now, let's focus on the gifts that come in the form of dollars and cents.

There are any number of famous people who focus their efforts on high-profile major charitable giving. These celebrities invest lots of time and energy in things like creating foundations, holding parties meant to raise funds that will help large groups of people, creating mass-media awareness, and so forth—all on behalf of a specific cause. That's all wonderful when the cause is worthy and the charity is both efficiently run and ethically operated. Those kinds of high-profile activities really are a great undertaking and a great topic for media coverage, because they inform lots of others about the important cause that the famous person is supporting, and they motivate other people to learn about the cause—and perhaps contribute, too.

But that's not the kind of charitable giving I'm talking about here.

Although I realize there are plenty of gentlepeople out there who *do* take part in this kind of prominent giving, either as an organizer or as a visible donor, I believe the gentlest people of all are those who give financial gifts anonymously, without anyone else ever knowing what they've given or under what circumstances the gift was made. This, I believe, is the very highest standard of giving. If we're truly gentlepeople, surely we are going to hold ourselves to the highest standard. That's what I want to urge you to do when it comes to your financial giving plan. I want you to make at least some part of your financial gift—large or small, it really doesn't matter—both regular and anonymous.

In theory, there's nothing *wrong* with giving in a high-profile way. And there are certainly some times when this is appropriate (for instance, to memorialize a loved one who has passed on). But if our aim is to give something that makes the biggest possible positive impact—and it should be—then we're going to find some way to give some of our material gifts anonymously.

So if there's a homeless shelter or a youth program or a home for abused women or any other worthy cause that you want to support financially, go ahead and give whatever you can, as regularly as you can—and why not do that without seeking out any formal public acknowledgment of your gift? That's how gentlepeople give: With the aim of pleasing their Creator rather than aiming to impress other human beings.

Winston Churchill, one of history's great gentlemen, once pointed out that we human beings make a living from what we get ... but we can only make a life from what we give. He was right. Follow his lead! Make a truly great life for yourself. Give financially to a worthy cause—as generously as you can manage, and for reasons that don't have anything to do with being recognized by others.

> ## WHAT DOES IT LOOK LIKE?
> What's the cause you care about most? How can you show it tangibly, whether with a small gift or a large one? Are you ready to follow through now?

CHAPTER TWENTY-EIGHT

Give Something Besides Money to Charity: Make Social Giving a Personal Priority.

*"The world is full of good people, but
if you can't find one, be one."*

—MOTHER TERESA

In the previous chapter, we looked at the issue of financial gifts to charitable causes, and we saw how the gentlest approach is to make these kinds of contributions without

133

seeking out any kind of public recognition for your gifts. In this chapter, I want to talk about a kind of contribution that absolutely *does* require that you make a public appearance—namely, charitable giving that has a social component, and that takes the form of a community effort that you make with other people. This is, I think, one of the best forms of gentle giving.

Gentlepeople know that true charity doesn't necessarily have anything to do with material gifts. They know that what matters is not how much we give, but how much love motivates the giving. And they also know that it's entirely possible to make a huge financial gift with absolutely no love motivating the decision to give. The gifts that matter most, both to the recipient and to the giver, are always the ones that come from the heart. Which is the reason I felt it was important to devote a chapter to the topic of what I'll call "social giving."

Social giving has nothing to do with social media. It's not an app. Social giving is giving that you do, not with money, but with your own time, energy, and focused attention, in the company of other real, live human beings.

That means that, whether or not you decided to give money to that homeless shelter you want to support, you find the time to volunteer there, in person, once a month—and you connect with other volunteers, and the people you're serving, in real

Give Something Besides Money to Charity

time. Not via a social media platform. Not over the phone. Not from a distance. In person.

Social giving is something you do with at least one other person .... that doesn't involve money changing hands ... and that benefits a cause that you personally feel is worthwhile because your communal action leaves the world a better place.

Gentlepeople know how important it is to give something back to the community that truly matters—and they also know that our time and attention are the most valuable commodities of all. That's why they don't stop with financial gifts. They make a personal commitment to engage in social giving on a regular basis. Why not follow their example?

Joining a neighborhood clean-up campaign. Manning a food bank. Helping your church or other spiritual community with an in-person outreach campaign that supports local young people who don't have great role models in their lives. Working door-to-door, with a partner, to raise funds for a cause you truly believe in. These are all examples of communal action in service of a good cause. And they're the kinds of things gentlepeople find the time to participate in, even though they are busy. That's why I'm going to strongly suggest here that you find a way to devote at least an hour of your time to social giving, once a month. If you stop to think about it, you'll realize that's really *not* a major time investment—and the payback you'll get from it in terms of contribution and connection is really priceless.

Doctor Martin Luther King Jr. once said, "Everybody can be great. Because anybody can serve. You don't have to have a college degree to serve. You don't have to make your subject and your verb agree to serve.... You don't have to know the second theory of thermodynamics in physics to serve. You only need a heart full of grace. A soul generated by love."

Truer words were never spoken—and gentlepeople are committed to living by those wise words.

WHAT DOES IT LOOK LIKE?

Is there a simple act of service that you could perform right now? What would happen if you did?

CHAPTER TWENTY-NINE

Be a Generational Translator: Learn How to Communicate With the Different Generations.

"Millennials, and the generations that follow, are shaping technology. This generation has grown up with computing in the palm of their hands. They are more socially and globally connected through mobile Internet devices than any prior generation. And they don't question; they just learn."

—BRIAN D. SMITH

Gentlepeople care about connecting with others in respectful, relevant, and impactful ways. They understand how important it is to interact effectively with people in ways that make them feel listened to and valued. Because they are committed, effective communicators, gentlepeople also understand that their perspective is not the only perspective. They know that their own generation's experience is not the only factor to be taken into account.

Five strikingly different generations will soon be sharing the national dialogue—an unprecedented state of affairs. Each deserves respect. Because they are committed to supporting respectful, effective, and sensitive communication across generations, gentlepeople make a point of familiarizing themselves with the main features of *each* generation's approach to communication—not just their own. And they go out of their way to help people from different generations understand what's really being said.

Here is a brief overview of the five generational groups ... and the very different assumptions and interaction strategies they are likely to employ.

TRADITIONALISTS

"A sense of personal responsibility and a commitment to honesty is characteristic of this generation. Those were

Be a Generational Translator

values bred into the young men and women coming of age at the time the war broke out. It's how they were raised."

—**Wesley Ko**

Meet the oldest of the five current generations: The Traditionalists, those born before 1946.

These people—many of whom are still working well into their seventies and eighties—lived through the Great Depression, World War II, and the Korean War. Their primary values are *dependability* and *sacrifice*. They are willing to put aside individual goals and aspirations for the good of the group. They are big on discipline, team play, and respect for authority. They tend to be conservative or even pessimistic, and they strive to think in the long term. They are the most resistant of the five generations to new forms of communications technology.

Traditionalists, like the Baby Boomers who followed them, are often seen by younger workers as "digital immigrants" because they did not grow up speaking the language of the digital world. To offer only the most obvious example, most Traditionalists took their time when it came to interacting via social media platforms. A fair number of them are still holding out against this powerful medium, despite the fact that it is now second nature and a potentially important economic resource to millions of younger people.

To interact effectively with Traditionalists, gentlepeople are prepared to appeal to the common good.

THE BABY BOOMERS

"The Boomers' biggest impact will be on eliminating the term 'retirement' and inventing a new stage of life ... the new career arc."

—**Rosabeth Moss Kanter**

The second-oldest of the five current generations would be the Baby Boomers, the workers born between 1946 and 1964. This large group includes most of the major decision makers who will be "calling the shots" between now and 2030. Their primary values are to *challenge limits* and *question everything*.

Baby Boomers are willing to confront authority when and as circumstances require, and they tend to have a stronger sense of social responsibility and a deeper understanding of the need for change and reform than the Traditionalists. As a general rule, Boomers are profoundly optimistic and willing to believe that any worthy goal can be achieved. They're generally less formal than Traditionalists, and they are more likely to focus on their own individual career goals than on team initiatives. They tend to be receptive to new communications technologies, although Baby Boomers, like Traditionalists, are often seen by younger workers as "digital immigrants." Most Boomers have now adapted to some of the tools of the social media revolution, which are effectively "hardwired" into the younger half of the nation.

To interact effectively with Baby Boomers, gentlepeople are prepared to identify a new and exciting goal that has not been attained before.

GENERATION X

"We're the middle children of history ... no purpose or place. We have no Great War, no Great Depression. Our great war is a spiritual war. Our great depression is our lives."

—From the movie *Fight Club*

"We watched our parents remain loyal to a company/ lifestyle/job only to be miserable at the end. Our strategy is to find a position that blends our family/work/ life into a cohesive entity that satisfies the monetary bank account and our karmic bank account."

—**Anonymous Gen X posting**

The group known as Generation X comprises those born between 1965 and 1976. More cynical than any of the other groups, these workers are likely to have little or no initial job loyalty. They need to be convinced to stick around. Their primary value is *independence.*

More than any other modern generation, their world is likely to be built around the concept of "looking out for number one." They expect to change jobs frequently and are deeply wary of promises made by authority figures. They are expert multitaskers who are comfortable with multiple communications technologies, and they adapt to new media platforms fairly easily. In any situation, they are likely to want to know what's in it for them. They tend to be more interested in short-term outcomes than in long-term initiatives.

To interact effectively with members of Generation X, gentle-people are prepared to prove to each individual Gen-Xer that what is under discussion is worth his/her valuable time, attention and/or money.

THE MILLENNIALS

"Millennials have a stronger sense of entitlement than older workers, according to a survey by CareerBuilder.com. The generation's greatest expectations: Higher

Be a Generational Translator

pay (74% of respondents); flexible work schedules (61%); a promotion within a year (56%); and more vacation or personal time (50%)."

—RON ALSOP

Now, meet the next of the five great current American generations: The group known as the Millennials, whose members were born between 1977 and 1997.

The Millennials are well educated (roughly 60% are college graduates). Their primary values are *fun* and *connection*. Many of these workers received significantly more parental attention and support in their youth than the Generation X workers did.

This generation grew up with computer games, the Internet, and the World Wide Web. They are not just "comfortable" with communications technology; communications technology forms an important part of their identity. They are tolerant, energetic, and demanding. They may have extremely short attention spans, thrive on visuals, prefer collaborative give-and-take to long lectures, and expect to see results more or less instantly. Millennials will make up roughly 50% of the US workforce by the year 2020, which means that ignoring their priorities and communication preferences is a big mistake.

To interact effectively with Millennials, gentlepeople are prepared to entertain them and provide some form of social stimulation ... because they seek to have fun and interact with others.

GENERATION 2020

"An overwhelming 37% of net kids have visited an online virtual world to play, socialize or meet friends according to eMarketer studies ... Generation 2020 will be the most multi-tasking generation to have ever existed, perfectly comfortable with multiple information streams and activities running at the same time, having a number of browser windows open at once, chatting via Instant Messaging (with) the TV on in the background while sending messages to friends."

—SOCIAL MACHINERY BLOG

It is largely Generation 2020's influence that has had virtual reality use skyrocketing in recent years, growing from 200,000 users worldwide in 2014 to a projected 171 million users in 2018—an increase of more than 850 times!

So far, we have learned about the Traditionalists, the Baby Boomers, Generation X, and the Millennials. Now meet the youngest of the five great American generations: Generation 2020. This highly educated generation, born around the year

2000, will enter the workforce by the end of the present decade, during a period when many Traditionalists will likely still be quite active. Analysts are still working out what to expect from this group. Words that are being used now to describe their values include the following:

Connected. Expect this group to be even more "wired" than the Millennials, because their entire lives have been spent under the powerful influence of the World Wide Web, online video games, social media, and virtual worlds like Second Life. As you read these words, they may well be updating their Facebook status, tweeting on Twitter, and posting content to Instagram—all while talking to a friend on Facetime.

Concerned. Members of Generation 2020 appear to be the most sensitive of all five groups to environmental problems and related social issues.

Careful. The recommendations of peers will carry enormous weight with this group. Expect these workers to think twice before making big purchase decisions. Unlike the Millennials, they are coming of age during a time of economic austerity. They are likely to seek value and be much more cautious with economic and career decisions, and thus share some important values with Traditionalists.

Collaborative. Like the Millennials, they are likely to be quite comfortable with collaborative endeavors, either face-to-face or virtual.

When in doubt, gentlepeople make a point of engaging with these younger people online—in ways that cater to their expressed tastes. They never embarrass them in front of their peers, online or otherwise!

To interact effectively with these young people, gentlepeople need to be prepared to understand, become part of, and respect their network. They celebrate Generation 2020's astonishing ability to interact and accomplish things within that network, and to leverage technology to achieve important goals.

A while back, a customer said to me, "Can you please e-mail that PowerPoint to me? I don't think I'm up to making the edits myself, but I'd like to have Billy help me with it." Billy was the customer's fourteen-year-old grandson! That's a perfect example of a (future) Generation 2020 worker pitching in to help out a Traditionalist. We should all get used to generating those kinds of stories. They show us the kind of exciting future we can all support as generational translators: Effective, collaborative, productive, and (of course) deeply respectful!

The presence of these five distinct generations leads to an unprecedented state of affairs—one that is already presenting major challenges in our society. Very often, conflict and miscommunication have their roots in generational differences.

Be a Generational Translator

Whether in your workplace, your family, or your community, it makes sense for you to understand the generational makeup of the group you're a part of and seek out opportunities to bridge the gaps that will doubtless make their presence felt.

> ## WHAT DOES IT LOOK LIKE?
>
> What would happen if you took a specific action to connect with someone from a different generation right now? Will you take the next step right now?

CHAPTER THIRTY

Be Authentic: Never Pretend to Be Someone You Aren't.

"Once you're who you really know yourself to be, you have no competition."

—Anonymous

Gentlepeople are authentic. That means they don't pretend to be someone other than who they are. They don't pretend to achieve things that they haven't. And they don't put on airs in an attempt to impress people. They learn from their own experiences and accept themselves in the moment, no matter what other people think of them.

I believe personal authenticity lies at the heart of all successful undertakings. Not some—all. I believe authenticity is the key to turning around any situation, even a dire one. And the wonderful thing I've discovered over the years is that *anyone* can be authentic, in any setting. All it takes is a personal decision to think with your heart as well as your head, a willingness to be honest about what you have learned and how you have learned it, and the certain knowledge that showing up and letting yourself be seen as you are is the foundation of any successful relationship.

Authenticity means admitting openly that you don't have all the answers and haven't learned all the lessons there are to learn in life. It means not pretending with yourself or anyone else that you're perfect. Authenticity flows from an open acknowledgment to the world at large that you are still learning *right now*—and that's okay.

One of the great traits of authentic leaders is that they freely admit when they have made mistakes, and they accept personal responsibility for the impact of their mistakes. This takes strength of character—and no small amount of personal vulnerability—but it is a universal trait of the gentlepeople I have come across over the years. When they make a mistake, they say so, right out loud. They don't pretend they're incapable of error. In

Be Authentic

addition, they know that making an honest, authentic acknowledgement of their own oversight or poor judgment in the past is a great bonding strategy in the present! People admire and respect gentlepeople who are willing and able to own up to their past decisions and actions when things didn't work out as well as they might have. We all admire people who have learned from setbacks and are willing to talk about those lessons.

One of my favorite examples of this kind of authenticity comes from NFL pro football hall of famer Fran Tarkenton, who launched a high-profile chain of restaurants back when he was still in his playing days. The restaurants failed. Instead of blaming his business advisors, which he could very easily have done, Tarkenton was authentic. He attributed the failure to his own lack of research in evaluating the project. "You can't rely on others to make you successful," he pointed out. "You have to be the one to figure out if there are customers that you can solve problems for, and if you can charge a rate that's both a great value to them and a way for you to make money. You need a good marketing platform. And you need to figure all that out before you go out and spend a lot of money." Tarkenton went on to start more than twenty successful businesses following his initial failure in the restaurant field—and he attributed his later extraordinary success to the lessons he learned from defeat.

"The only way you learn, in football or in business," he

pointed out, "is by losing." That's not only true—it's the sound of a great leader being humble and authentic. And that's a sound that people love to hear!

> ## WHAT DOES IT LOOK LIKE?
>
> What would happen if you took full responsibility for something that didn't turn out as well as you hoped it would? What's the lesson to carry with you as move forward?

CHAPTER THIRTY-ONE

Be Tactful in Your Speech: Use the Best Words You Can Think of, not the Worst.

"The right word fitly spoken is a precious rarity."

—John Boyle O'Reilly

Gentlepeople don't use language to hurt other people. It's not how they operate. As the old adage goes, if they don't have anything nice to say, they don't say

The Gentle Life

anything at all. This is one of the defining characteristics of a gentleperson.

Tactful speech is nothing more or less than the verbal expression of the Golden Rule. Following this rule as it applies to our speech simply means noticing when we are tempted to say words to someone else that we ourselves wouldn't want to hear and taking time to think of something else to say—or resolving to say nothing at all.

Using tactful language at all times, with all people, may seem like an old-fashioned notion, given the popularity of insults, trash talk, and online bullying in our contemporary discourse. But it's a standard that I believe is worth remembering, noticing, and upholding—one that can help us to harness the extraordinary power of the written and spoken word to bring people together rather than tear them apart.

Over 150 years ago, Abraham Lincoln—a great man who was held in contempt by millions of his countrymen, a gentleman who appears during his final, tumultuous years never to have had a harsh word for even his fiercest critics—shared some sage advice on the too-often-neglected art of selecting one's words carefully, in such a way as to avoid causing hurt feelings or damage to another person's self-esteem. His words are worth considering closely today—and if being a gentleperson matters to you, I would ask you to consider them closely the next time you find yourself tempted to say something harsh, something you wouldn't want someone saying to or about you: "Tact is the ability to describe others just as they see themselves."

If there is a better role model for tactful, gentle, effective speech, both spoken and written, than our nation's 16th President, I would like to know who that person is so I can learn more about him or her!

> ## WHAT DOES IT LOOK LIKE?
> Can you imagine speaking to someone in your life in a way that consistently expresses your confidence in their ability to achieve what they have set out to do—and to become the person they wish to be? What would happen in that relationship if you embraced such a commitment?

CHAPTER THIRTY-TWO

Don't Talk About People Behind Their Backs: Work It out With Them in Person or Don't Talk About It at All.

"The old proverb about sticks and stones is wrong. A broken bone can heal, but the wound from a single hurtful word can take a lifetime to heal, or perhaps never heal at all."

—**Mike Cleary**

The Gentle Life

In the previous chapter, we looked at the importance of speaking tactfully when you're engaging with another person. That discussion covers the question of how we should interact when we're face to face, but it doesn't cover the extremely common situation of people talking trash about those who aren't in the same room with them.

Unfortunately, we live in a time when disparaging people who aren't around to defend themselves has become something very close to a national pastime. So it seems important to include a chapter about how gentlepeople approach the question of backbiting.

Here's how they approach it: They don't do it!

This means gentlepeople often have to exclude themselves from conversations, because so much of our daily interaction—and particularly our daily workplace interaction—is based on scoring social points by saying harsh things about absent parties! This is ungentle behavior. When gentlepeople notice that they are being drawn into it, they find a reason to redirect the conversation or disengage and do something else.

Backbiting is so common now that many people hardly even realize that it's happening. They have no concept of what this problem even is. They simply assume that this destructive communication pattern is how people interact with one another—saving up the things that they know would offend or hurt an individual for the times when that person isn't around to hear. They think that's normal, everyday speech. It's not. It's attack speech.

So, for instance, let's say you think someone you work with has made a mistake on the job, and you don't take the opportunity to tell that person, tactfully and in private, what you think happened and how it affected you. If you are more than happy to share your opinions with his or her peers when the person is out sick for the day, that's backbiting.

By the same token, if you think someone in your family has mistreated you, and you tell everyone in the family *except* that person how you feel, that's backbiting.

Or say you feel that a friend has let you down in some way, and you decide to send texts to all your mutual acquaintances detailing just how devastated you are, and why—but you *don't* make any effort to reach out to the friend in question so you can sit down and try to work things out. That's backbiting, too.

Gentlepeople follow a simple rule in these situations. They either speak privately with the individual in question and try to work things out ... or they don't take part in the conversation at all. Yes, this means they don't take part in the destructive, massively popular spectator sport called gossip. The guiding principle here is very simple: If the words in question reflect a problem that needs to be worked out, then gentlepeople go to the source and work out the problem. They don't disparage the character or actions of others in their social circle for the sake of entertainment.

Public figures such as actors, musicians, or politicians may be an exception of sorts. They knew the job was dangerous when they took it! But when it comes to the way we communicate about the people in our working lives, our family lives, and our communities, backbiting is toxic and destructive. That's why gentlepeople avoid it, no matter how widely accepted it becomes.

Yes, some people can make backbiting seem entertaining, and even make it addictive. It's the coin of the realm in some social circles. But here's a question to consider if you're ever tempted to participate in a social circle that's based on backbiting (of which there are plenty): *Don't you think someone who will talk trash TO you will eventually talk trash ABOUT you?*

> ## WHAT DOES IT LOOK LIKE?
> Why do you think people talk disparagingly about others when they're not around? How could you redirect or graciously decline the opportunity to participate in such conversations? What would happen as a result?

CHAPTER THIRTY-THREE

Be a Teacher: Share What You've Learned.

"The mediocre teacher tells. The good teacher explains. The superior teacher demonstrates. The great teacher inspires."

—WILLIAM ARTHUR WARD

Gentlepeople, I've noticed, are not just lifelong learners. They're lifelong teachers, too.

That doesn't mean that they force their opinions on others, and it certainly doesn't mean that they assume they've figured out everything important in life. But it does mean that they recognize teaching moments when they come along, and they act on those teaching moments.

A teaching moment is a moment when you sense that someone who is open to your guidance is ready and willing to embrace a lesson that you've already learned. This person doesn't have to be your protégé. It could be a nine-year-old you just met in a park, a ninety-year old you met in a supermarket, or anyone in between. Teaching moments are what keep humanity on the move, learning, and growing. We all have a responsibility to notice them and take full advantage of them. Gentlepeople seem to be particularly adept at spotting them, starting a discussion, and helping to turn that discussion into an opportunity for positive development. This can be a tremendously fulfilling and rewarding experience for both teacher and learner. When I was a boy, my father, a true gentleman, often said to me, "Everything I know, I've learned—and everything I've learned, I share." Those words have always stayed with me, and I've tried my best to live up to them.

Teaching moments have a way of coming along spontaneously. Not long ago, a friend told me the inspiring story of a high school teacher whose best student—I'll call her Maria—had stopped participating in class in her usual enthusiastic, curious way. This wasn't just a one-time occurrence; it kept up for the better part of a week. Finally the teacher, whom I'll call

Tim, asked Maria to stay behind after class so they could have a private talk. During that talk, Tim asked his student to share whether there was some kind of problem at home that they should discuss.

Maria gave him a blank look. The conversation went nowhere for the next few minutes. Maria denied there was any problem and seemed eager to leave as soon as possible. Tim couldn't seem to get her to open up about what was causing the obvious changes in her behavior. After several fruitless rounds of evasive small talk, Maria simply excused herself, stood up and began to make her way to the door.

Tim noticed a deep sadness in her expression before she turned her back on him.

At that moment, he spotted his teaching moment, though if you'd asked him thirty seconds earlier whether he had anything to teach Maria, he would have had to have answered "No." But in that instant, he said, "Look, you know and I know there is something wrong here. What you may not know, though, is that there really are people in this world you can trust, people who will respect your privacy. And I promise you, Maria, I am one of those people."

It was as though the whole world had decided that it was time to hold absolutely still. Maria's hand, which had been reaching for the door, froze in place for a long moment. Then she withdrew it slowly, turned around, and returned to her seat at her teacher's desk. She looked Tim in the eye, and he noticed that the sad expression on her face had deepened, and that Maria's eyes had rimmed with tears.

"Okay," she said. "Here's what's going on. I'm in trouble."

As it turned out, Maria was pregnant. She had no idea what to do. She didn't trust any of the adults in her life to help her make the right decision. And she certainly didn't trust the high-school senior who had slept with her. She begged the teacher to keep his word and keep their conversation private.

Tim assured her that he would be as good as his word. Then he asked her how he could help. Maria broke down in sobs, then collected herself and talked at length about what had happened and why she felt she could tell no one, not even her closest friends at school. Tim listened for the next half hour. That, he realized, was what Maria really needed most at that moment: Someone to listen.

Maria ended up deciding to have her baby and pursue the possibility of finding a married couple interested in adoption. She took advantage of Tim's offer of help in telling her family what had happened, and she eventually accepted his help in dealing with the social service agencies that would assist her in locating the right couple. But that's not really the point of this story. The point is that Tim saw the teaching moment and acted on it.

The critical moment was the one when he chose to focus with certainty on the lesson he knew, deep down, that Maria needed most: *There really are people in this world you can trust, even when you are feeling lost and confused and afraid. You just have to look for them.*

It was probably the most important lesson he ever shared with one of his students ... and it had nothing to do with a textbook. I think we can all be gentle teachers like Tim. The key to doing so lies in learning to recognize your own teaching moments!

> ## WHAT DOES IT LOOK LIKE?
> Do you think listening could be a powerful teaching tool for someone in your life? What would happen if you listened deeply to them?

CHAPTER THIRTY-FOUR

Drink Deeply From Good Books—Especially the Bible: Books Are Among Life's Greatest Treasures.

"Your word is a lamp to my feet and a light to my path."

—Psalm 119:105

The legendary UCLA basketball coach John Wooden, one of the truly great gentlemen of his era, took just as much pride in developing character as he did in developing basketball skills. Among the powerful pieces of advice he made a point of sharing with the young men he coached was this injunction: "Drink deeply from good books—especially the Bible." I can think of no better way to improve on Wooden's habitual instruction to his players, so I am reproducing it verbatim here. If he felt this advice was worth sharing season after season, decade after decade, with each and every one of the players he took on at UCLA, who am I to dispute the point?

It is not always in fashion to recommend that people read the Bible, but my experience is that doing so requires no apology. This remarkable book is not only the central pillar of the Western ethical, literary, and philosophical traditions, but it is also an opportunity for constant and beneficial self-reflection. Whether you consider yourself a Christian, a Jew, a Muslim, an atheist, an agnostic, or you adopt some other category, you will *definitely* benefit from exposing yourself to the ideas in this book ... and that's something that can't be said for every book on the shelf. I'm certainly not suggesting you should *limit* yourself to the Bible, and neither was Coach Wooden. When it comes to great books, there's lots of variety, whether you enjoy reading history, novels, philosophy, religion, self-help books, or all of the above. But I am saying, without hesitation or embarrassment, that the Bible should also be on everyone's reading list. And I can't imagine a gentleperson who would exclude it from such a list.

Drink Deeply From Good Books—Especially the Bible

If you happen to be a believer, reading the Bible will strengthen your bond with your Creator and deepen your sense of purpose in life and your ability to contribute to the society within which you live. You will likely take special comfort and instruction from verses such as Joshua 1:8: "Study this Book of Instruction continually. Meditate on it day and night so you will be sure to obey everything written in it. Only then will you prosper and succeed in all you do."

If you happen to be a nonbeliever or are simply skeptical about religious matters, reading the Bible will give you some helpful perspective. This perspective is crucial for any open-minded person who is faced with a powerful and unavoidable question: *Why is the Bible the most influential book in human history?*

At the very least, avoiding such a question leads to a gap in one's education. Coach Wooden didn't believe in leaving such gaps unfilled, and neither do I.

You don't have to believe, as I do, that the Scriptures are the revealed Word of God in order to believe that the Bible has had an extraordinary and enduring impact on people all over the world. Surely exploring this great book cover to cover at least once will bring you some fundamental insights on the reasons for its extraordinary impact—and indeed on the human condition itself.

Coach Wooden was known to insist to his players that making

a habit of reading great books, especially the Bible, would "make you a little better than you are." This was not always a popular message among young men in their teens and twenties who had arrived at UCLA with the single goal of becoming great basketball players, and it was not always well received during the tumultuous years of the 1960s and 1970s, when traditionalist approaches such as Wooden's were under heavy fire on many of the nation's campuses, including UCLA. But he never stopped sharing that message, and I believe he was right not to do so.

Gentlepeople don't force their beliefs on others, but they don't overlook learning opportunities, either, and the Bible presents humanity with deep and profound opportunities for learning. Take advantage of those opportunities! Read it cover to cover, at least once in your life.

In fact, it would be better for you to read the Bible far more than that. Over 30 years ago, while attending a memorial service for a friend's father, I was challenged by his life story as it was told during the service. Reading the Bible had changed his life's direction from being a successful middle-aged business owner to becoming the pastor of a small church in St. Louis. The speaker challenged us to start reading the Bible through every year, as the businessman-turned-pastor had done. I accepted his challenge, and this December will mark the 31st time I have read

Drink Deeply From Good Books—Especially the Bible

through the Bible in a year. This practice has changed my life! That's why I'm asking you to consider doing it, too.

> ## WHAT DOES IT LOOK LIKE?
>
> Have you ever read the Bible all the way through? What might you gain if you did? What's one other book that you aspire to read, and why?

CHAPTER THIRTY-FIVE

Respect Your Parents: No Matter How Old They Are.

"Never use the sharpness of your tongue on the one who taught you to speak."

—**Anonymous**

The columnist John Rosemond of the Tribune News Service wrote an inspiring column recently that reminded me how vitally important the value of respect for parents is. The column, which ran on January 1, 2017, bears the attention-getting headline "Your Kids Should Not Be the Most Important," and it begins as follows:

> I recently asked a married couple who had three kids, none of whom are yet teens, "Who are the most important people in your family?"
>
> Like all good moms and dads of this brave millennium, they answered, "Our kids!"
>
> "Why?" I then asked. "What is it about your kids that gives them that status?" And like all good moms and dads of this brave new millennium, they couldn't answer the question other than to fumble with appeals to emotion. So I answered the question for them: "There is no reasonable thing that gives your children that status. I went on to point out that many if not most of the problems they're having with their kids—typical stuff these days—are the result of treating their children as if they, their marriage, and the family exist because of the kids ... when in fact it is the other way around. Their kids exist because of them and their marriage, and thrive because they have created a stable family. Furthermore, without them, their kids wouldn't eat well, have the nice clothing they wear, live in the nice home in which they live, enjoy the great vacations they enjoy, and so on.

Respect Your Parents

Rosemond is absolutely on point here, and he is pointing us all toward an important life lesson—one that is not always popular or intuitive for younger generations, but that has been, in my experience, a consistent core value of gentlepeople: *Parents are the engine of the family unit, and they should always be honored and respected as such by the children they raise.*

Gentlepeople know that observing the age-old injunction to "Honor thy father and thy mother" is and always will be a core element of a healthy, functioning society. This is a principle that we ignore at our peril—one that transcends questions of age, race, and culture. It is universally applicable and should be universally reinforced. Parents are the center of the family unit.

This is not to say that the children or grandchildren or great-grandchildren within a given family should be neglected or disrespected—far from it! But it is to say that when we follow the (common) current trend of imagining that the children in a family unit have, deserve, or could possibly benefit from always being at the center of the family's decision-making process, we are making a grave mistake. The only way we can possibly give our children, grandchildren, and great-grandchildren all the attention, support, and resources they deserve is by recognizing the special bond and the special responsibility that exists in the relationship between parent and child ... and accepting that we will only weaken that bond and make life more difficult for

The Gentle Life

our kids if we let them imagine that they are the center of the universe. They're not. Believing that they are is not a healthy outlook for kids or for parents, and it certainly doesn't create a viable structure for any functioning family unit. Gentlepeople, I believe, know that.

A tip of the hat to Rosemond for taking a stand on this issue, and for reminding us all that we have an obligation to respect our parents, no matter how old we are and no matter how old they are. As he points out, in an army, the most important person is always going to be the general; in a company, the most important person is always going to be the CEO or president; and in a family, the most important person is going to be the parent. That's a simple fact of human life, and whether or not it is fashionable to embrace it, gentlepeople live by that principle.

Of course, one's place in the family can't be claimed or maintained through simply stating one's right to it. Great parenting is characterized by service—not servility—and it can be a hard balance to find. Those who do find that balance ultimately impart the sorts of structure, direction, and clarity to the family that lead to positive developments for everyone. Too often, though, parents abdicate their responsibility by raising their children in a way that has everyone forfeiting priceless opportunities for learning.

Let me attempt to illustrate these things through a story. A number of years ago, I had the experience of delivering a less-than-stellar performance review to an employee who wasn't holding up his end of the bargain. The next day, I received a call expressing frustration that I hadn't given him a generous raise. I took this call, not from the employee himself, but from his mother! Despite never having stepped foot in our offices, she was sure that her son deserved a large pay increase.

I don't know much about that young gentleman's upbringing, but based on that call, it wouldn't surprise me to learn that he was consistently being told that he could do no wrong, that he was a champion just for showing up, and so on. I have a hunch that opportunities for him to listen to criticism and learn from failures—which would have allowed him to identify his unique abilities, correct his behavior where necessary, and improve himself—may have been passed over.

The point is, we shortchange our children by placing them on the family pedestal. Eventually, they will have experiences out in the world that send them toppling from that place. How will they respond? What will they learn? And who will they talk through the valuable lessons with? Sadly, if their parents have not provided them with space to process what they're learning through their failures as well as their successes, these are vital discussions that may never take place.

THE GENTLE LIFE

> ## WHAT DOES IT LOOK LIKE?
>
> What's one way that you can demonstrate care for your parents—or for your children—related to what you've seen in this chapter? What would happen if you took action right now?

CHAPTER THIRTY-SIX

Build a Plan for the Future: No Matter How Old You Are.

"You must have long-term goals to keep you from being frustrated by short-term failures."

—**Charles C. Noble**

My dad used to say, "We're too soon old, and too late smart!" That remark always made me laugh, because he was a pretty smart guy—even though it took me a while to realize that. One of the things this saying reminds me of is that it's never too late for any of us to set up a smart plan for the rest of our lives. This is something that the gentlepeople I know do consistently: They orient their lives toward the future. No matter how old they get, they're always setting new goals, always planning out the next phase of the journey that will lead them closer to being the kind of person they want to become. They hold it as a matter of principle to regard themselves (as I have noted elsewhere in this book) as works in progress. And they create written plans based on that principle.

With that idea in mind, I have updated my dad's saying. The version I share with people now is, "No matter how old we happen to be, we're smart enough right now to make a great plan for the rest of our lives."

If you're old enough to have clear opinions about what you like and what you don't like, then you're old enough to do what the gentlepeople I love and respect the most have done: Be bold enough to plan your own future—in writing! This is an essential element of what I have called the gentle life: Planning for the best and making it a reality in your life, regardless of your chronological age.

My challenge to you on this front is pretty simple: I want you to follow the example of the most inspiring gentlepeople I know by taking the time to write out your very own 25-year plan for

Build a Plan for the Future

the next phase of your life. I want you to commit to doing this even if (especially if) you're not certain that you've got 25 years to work with!

Gentlepeople aren't stuck the past. They always look ahead to the future. And I want you to follow their lead. I want you to commit to doing more things—and more exciting things—over the next quarter-century than you've ever done before. Once you set up a long-term plan, in writing, you're much more likely to do those things, because getting them down in black and white means you're doing a better job of visualizing and planning for those precious years, which means you're much more likely to take action. So start writing! Get it all down! I propose four main categories for the people I work with on this exciting topic, yielding a total of twenty powerful goals to pursue. I ask them:

- What five specific things would you want to be sure you have experienced or accomplished in your life five years from now?
- Ten years from now?
- Twenty years from now?
- Twenty-five years from now?

Don't be afraid of putting big goals on this list. Climbing mountains has been a personal favorite of mine when composing this list—and one I'm proud to be able to say that I've followed

The Gentle Life

through on. But what's on my list doesn't really matter. What matters is what's on your list!

I'm part of a futurist group in California called Abundance 360. It's a group of scientists, physicians, and business leaders dedicated to thinking big about the future. And we get together for three or four days in Beverly Hills, California, once a year, to study the latest, greatest, most audacious things that are happening around the world, from artificial intelligence to robotics to conflict resolution to sustainable economic development on a global scale. It's one of the most exciting things I've ever done in my life! One thing I've learned from that group is that you need some audaciousness to get the most out of a big idea. And let's face it, writing your very own 25-year-plan is audacious.

If you plan to live into your seventies, eighties, or nineties, and you don't make it, so what? You still need to plan to do great things. I have a friend who's planning for what he's going to do when he's 110 years old. I'm making the same kind of written plan. Yes, we may not get there, but we'll come up with some big ideas and some bold initiatives along the way. We'll make some big contributions. And we'll live life to the fullest in the years that we do have! That's what thinking big is all about. And that's the way I want to challenge you to think as this book nears its close. Set up your own audacious, positive 25-year plan ... in writing!

> # WHAT DOES IT LOOK LIKE?
>
> What would happen if you made bold plans to pursue a handful of audacious and worthwhile goals over the next 25 years? What's the next step, and when will you take it?!

To help spur your thinking, I'd like to share my own 25-year plan here.

Tom Klobucher's 25-Year Plan

January 2010 to January 2035 (Age 95)

- Choose the age that suits me best and live like it. (Mine is age fifty.)
- Be a lifetime learner and always share what I learn.
- Be a trusted adviser to my family, friends, and associates.
- Always be positive.
- Show up on time.
- Always say please and thank you.
- Do what I say I will do.
- Build and practice a great trust in God.
- Walk and pray with my wife every morning.

The Gentle Life

- Pray for my family and for others every morning and evening.
- Read the Bible through every year. (Thirty-one times so far)
- Keep writing books. (This is my eighth!)
- Always have positive small groups and Mastermind teams to challenge me and keep a future focus.
- Be a positive "sage" to younger people.
- Be a man of faith and prayer.
- Always keep working. ("If you rest...you rust."—Cliff Raad)
- Laugh often and enjoy life...be a joyful, gentle person.
- Be future-based in everything I do and say.
- Watch little or no TV.
- Be generous and cultivate an attitude of gratitude—be grateful.
- Be a model father, grandfather, great-grandfather and a fully ENGAGED man.
- Be happy and thankful—not grumpy.
- Wash and dress well every day.
- Celebrate and build my relationship with my wife and our family.
- Be audacious and bold in all that I do.
- Hang out with younger people and be a mentor.

Build a Plan for the Future

- Be a generational coach.
- Model what I write about.
- Be a transformational leader in all that I do. Life is not a transaction…it is a transformation. Always be transforming!
- Keep up with current technology.
- Live life and have no regrets.
- Live each year as if it were a precious resource. It is!
- Practice lifetime growth—learn and share with people from other backgrounds.
- Live exponentially.
- Live life for the long term…and for eternity.

CHAPTER THIRTY-SEVEN

Be a Polite Driver: Put a Human Face on Everyone Around You.

"The driver that you have to sell on safety shouldn't be driving."

—Kyle Petty

A few years ago, a father was driving down Interstate 40 in Albuquerque, New Mexico. Along for the ride were his 7-year-old son and 4-year-old daughter. Just as the father set out to maneuver toward an exit, another car abruptly cut across traffic, prompting the father to exchange heated words with the driver of the out-of-control vehicle.

That's when the unthinkable happened: The driver who had endangered other travelers on the interstate by weaving through traffic became enraged, drew a gun, and fired several shots into the concerned father's car. One of those bullets struck his 4-year-old daughter in the head, resulting in her death.

The shooter fled the scene, but was ultimately found by police and charged with multiple felonies.

The grief-stricken father had this to say about his late daughter during an interview: "She was so proud to tell people she just turned 4. She just started school two days ago. She was very bright and very smart."

* * *

I'm sure you agree with me that tragedies like the one described above should never happen. The searing pain associated with the loss of a young child is incalculable, and it certainly dwarfs the perceived offense caused by whatever words were exchanged leading up to the shooting.

If you're reading this book, I doubt whether I have to convince you of these things. And yet, I think you may be surprised to learn that the extreme incidents that we typically associate with the term "road rage" may only be the tip of a massive iceberg that threatens everyone on the road at all times. I was frankly surprised at what I learned while researching these things.

Consider this:

- In recent years, there have been about 35,000 deaths per year resulting from accidents on the road, and two-thirds of those deaths—over 23,000 per year—resulted from aggressive driving.
- Shockingly, over 80% of drivers have exhibited road rage of some form in the last year, meaning that they have intentionally and aggressively tried to harm or inconvenience other drivers.
- The types of aggressive driving associated with road rage constitute a far greater danger to travelers than drunk drivers do. (Drunk driving is a factor in about 10,000 deaths per year.)
- Common road rage behaviors include blocking another vehicle from changing lanes, running another vehicle off the road, or otherwise seeking to get even with or thwart another driver.

Honesty compels me to admit that I've not always been thought of by those who know me as the calmest driver around, and the statistics clearly indicate that most of us have engaged in one of these behaviors in the not-too-distant past. If you reflect carefully on your own driving in recent months, perhaps you'll realize that—maybe in a moment of exhaustion or stress—you engaged another vehicle or driver in one of the ways described above. If that's the case, and if no significant harm resulted from it, count yourself privileged! This is a great opportunity to learn an important lesson and commit to driving differently in the future.

Those who approach driving as a competition—who weave in and out of lanes as if they were playing a video game, or who get into shouting matches with other drivers—actually face a strong likelihood of eventually causing unspeakable harm to another person or themselves.

So what's the alternative?

I think part of the solution lies in putting a human face on the too-often nameless individuals who travel on the same roads we do. Most of them are just like we are: People who are sometimes tired or discouraged, folks who are just trying to get to work to provide for those they love or get home safely. When they make mistakes—and we all make mistakes out on the road—I'd like to think they generally make them with the best of intentions.

And then, often there are children in the vehicles around us. How do we feel about the children who have been entrusted into our care? Wouldn't it make sense to remember that others feel exactly the same about every child we encounter throughout our days—including those in the vehicles around us?

If you've read much of what I've written in the past, you know that I have a tendency to make bold plans and set audacious goals. The more I think about our responsibility to other drivers on the road, the more I value the opportunity to promote the safety of others in everything I do behind the wheel. Would you join me in an effort to massively reduce the death toll associated with aggressive driving, which currently hovers well above 20,000 deaths per year?

> ## WHAT DOES IT LOOK LIKE?
>
> What does the way you drive say about you? Is it obvious that you value the lives of other travelers—or should people be afraid to make a mistake around you because you're likely to fly off the handle? What would it look like to treat other people on the road the same way you want them to treat you and the people you love the most?

A FINAL WORD

Be a Witness—Notice and Praise Gentle Behavior Whenever You Encounter It

"Keep a little fire burning, however small, however hidden."

—Cormac McCarthy

In this book, I've shared what I believe are the hallmarks of the gentle life. It's a wonderful way of life, one that becomes more easily recognizable with the passage of time—if you keep noticing, reinforcing, and celebrating its key ideas.

The Gentle Life

My final challenge to you is a simple one: Help and encourage others to learn to live this way.

Discuss the principles you have learned about here with your friends and family. Share this book's message with your pastor, priest, or other spiritual leader—and ask for his or her ideas on how best to spread this book's message. Most important of all, *notice* people who act in accordance with the principles I've shared with you, and celebrate those people at every possible opportunity.

When you notice someone giving up a seat on a crowded bus, or reaching out to act as a role model for a young person who's in trouble, or de-escalating a pointless conflict, or following through on any of the other guidelines you've read about here, *say something positive to that person, right out loud, right away.* Let the person know that you noticed what they were doing and you appreciate it. This, too, is a critical responsibility of gentlepeople: Recognizing and encouraging one of their own.

Let the person know how much it means to you to have found a kindred spirit. Let him or her know why you believe being a gentleperson matters. Let him or her know how much you appreciate their willingness to set a good example for friends, family, and society as a whole. And keep the conversation about gentle behavior alive!

This is how gentlepeople encourage and share the most important life lessons, not just in their own time, but for generations to

Be a Witness

come. They make it a point the keep the gentle conversation alive in the present tense ... and they encourage others to do the same.

I've written this book with the aim of starting a local, national, and global conversation in praise of gentle values. If you've benefited from that conversation, please continue it! Whenever you see tangible evidence of gentle behavior that improves the quality of just one person's life, make a point of celebrating that behavior right away so that the same positive behavior can be repeated again and again and enrich the lives of many more people!

Please help me to spread this message. And thank you in advance for making a gentler world possible.

> ## WHAT DOES IT LOOK LIKE?
>
> Can you identify one admirable act you recently saw someone else perform? Are you in a position to make contact with that individual and let them know how much you appreciated what they did? What would happen if you did this right now?

APPENDIX A

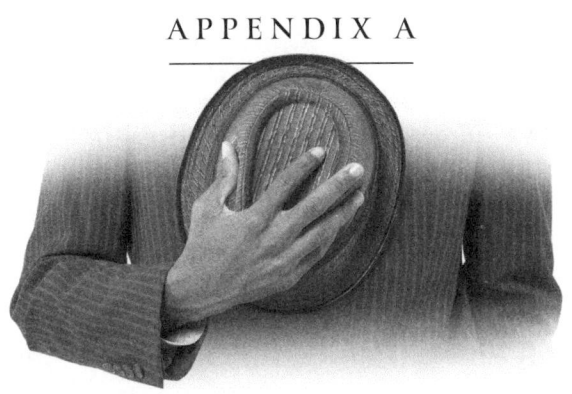

Characteristics of a Transformational Mentor

Naphtali Hoff's wonderful article, "Being an Abundant Mentor," appeared in the *SmartBlog on Leadership* on January 13, 2016. The article described Hoff's discussions with various managers in search of the qualities that set apart a truly great mentor. Hoff's article identified the following characteristics:

1. **Being available:** Having an open door policy when it comes to communicating with the mentee informally as well as coaching him or her in regular scheduled meetings.
2. **Being consistent:** Always applying the same standards

and principles when problem solving and brainstorming with the mentee—as well as not playing favorites by placing the interests of one mentee above another.

3. **Being accountable:** Following through on commitments—and not making commitments lightly in the first place.
4. **Treating mentees as adults:** Establishing a solid peer-to-peer relationship with the mentee, and never talking down to him or her.
5. **Being authentic:** Shooting straight from the shoulder, not putting on an act, and not engaging in unnecessary drama within the relationship. If the mentor can't share the truth with the mentee and vice versa, there is no meaningful relationship and no potential for growth on either side.
6. **Being a good listener:** Engaging in active listening—the kind of listening that replays, as necessary, what the other person has just said to make it clear that the speaker has been heard and understood.
7. **Not imposing solutions:** Using life experience to begin, but not to dominate, meaningful discussions with the mentee about how to move forward in any area mutually identified as important to the mentee. In other words, the mentor is a coach, not a boss.

Characteristics of a Transformational Mentor

8. **Having one's head in the game:** Being engaged, patient, pragmatic, and focused on appropriate opportunities, both in the short term and in the long term.

9. **Practicing abundance thinking:** Focusing on what is possible, not just what is difficult; focusing on what is next, not just what has happened in the past; focusing on gratitude, not despair; and focusing on ways that everyone can win, not just on those games where victories come at someone else's expense. This habit of cultivating gratitude and engaging in abundance thinking is one of the most important characteristics of an effective mentor. For more on abundance thinking, which is a lifelong mastery topic, consider this powerful quote from Alexandra Katehakis: "Summoning gratitude is a sure way to get our life back on track. Opening our eyes to affirm gratitude grows the garden of our inner abundance, just as standing close to a fire eventually warms our heart." All the mentors who really made a difference in my life modeled this ninth characteristic. I have tried to model it, in turn, for those whom I've mentored.

10. **Being personally validating:** Being committed to the mentee's fullest, most exciting possibility, the best possible version of himself or herself; being committed to transformation, to helping the mentee learn and grow

and eventually take on the role of mentor for someone else. The best mentors are never out to build their own resume or secure short-term political advantage. They are in the game for the team and for the long haul. They are committed to ongoing personal growth—both their own and the mentee's.

If your personal aim is to become an effective transformational mentor—and if you've made it this far into the book, I'm certainly hoping that it is—then my challenge to you is to practice all ten of these characteristics until they become second nature to you in your interactions with those you choose to mentor. Become a personal role model in all ten of these areas—and watch the magic that results!

APPENDIX B

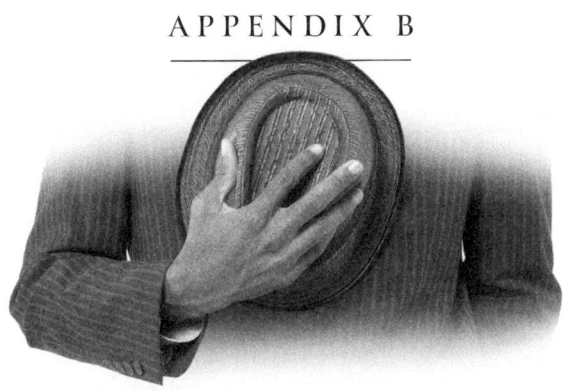

Ten Transformational, Life-Giving Steps for a Positive, Happy, and Engaged Life

Here are ten simple steps you can take, starting today, that will make you a more positive, happy, and connected person.

1. Watch your diet, eat healthy foods, and eat less.
2. Sleep seven to eight hours per night.
3. Be sure to drink plenty of water daily (not so much coffee and soft drinks). Hydration is one of the keys to health.

The Gentle Life

4. Exercise every day. Walk a minimum of one mile.
5. Turn off the TV—or get rid of it altogether!
6. Always be learning—read books. Read at least one book per month.
7. Always be focused on the future—not the past.
8. Be engaged in every situation and have a grateful, positive attitude.
9. Join or start a transformational group that will inspire and challenge you.
10. Seize every opportunity to build an attitude of gratitude.

Other Books by Tom Klobucher

The Great Workplace Revolution takes the reader through the twelve essential strategies for creating a great place to work—and provides the tools to better understand and leverage the unique giftedness of the five distinct workplace generations that will be working together in this most exciting decade!

 *The Great Workplace Transformation* is a learning parable that shows business leaders how to hire and retain the most creative, loyal, and growth-driven employees, transforming their workplaces into powerhouses that thrive in the present multi-generational environment!

The Tailor's Son is an authentic American story on classic themes: Father, son, and the healing power of belief. Here Tom takes a loving look back at the perils of youth, the distance that can arise between father and son, and the potential for reconciliation and positive change.

 *Retirement: The Best Is Yet to Come* provides the retirement roadmap for the time of your life! What is the secret to a successful retirement? Tom shares twenty-five bold steps to a happy, positive, fulfilled and engaged retirement!

Transformational Relationships is a learning tool for every generation that traces our positive transformational relationships—from early childhood to our senior years—and prepares us for our very best life!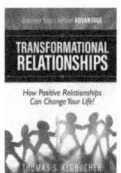

 *Marriage: The Time of Your Life* helps readers discover the great treasure of an engaged, transformational marriage—and to live happily ever after!

Tales of Gratitude is a collection of positive short stories with happy endings that will inspire thankfulness in the young and the young at heart.

WANT TO LEARN MORE?

Please join us at www.amazon.com/author/thomasklobucher

or www.talkswithtom.com

Tom Klobucher, Founder, CEO, Author & Speaker
Thomas Interiors, Inc.
476 Brighton Drive
Bloomingdale, IL 60108
630 980 4200
tomk@thomasinteriors.com